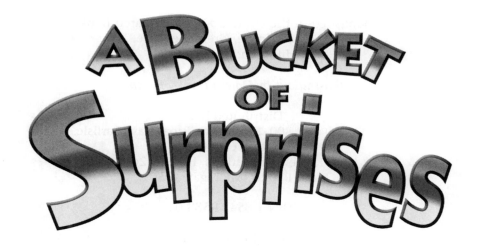

A Bucket of Surprises

J. John & Mark Stibbe

MONARCH
BOOKS

Mill Hill, London & Grand Rapids, Michigan

First published in the UK in 2002 by Monarch Books,
Concorde House, Grenville Place,
Mill Hill, London NW7 3SA.

Illustrations by Darren Harvey Regan

Distributed by:
UK: STL, PO Box 300, Kingstown Broadway, Carlisle,
Cumbria CA3 0QS;
USA: Kregel Publications, PO Box 2607
Grand Rapids, Michigan 49501.

ISBN 1 85424 588 0

British Library Cataloguing Data
A catalogue record for this book is available
from the British Library.

Book design and production for the publishers by
Gazelle Creative Productions Ltd,
Concorde House, Grenville Place, Mill Hill, London NW7 3SA.

Acknowledgements

We are indebted to all those who have been kind enough to send us some great stories, especially since the publication of our first volume, *A Box of Delights*.

We are also indebted to all those who originally came up with the stories in this present volume. It is absolutely impossible to trace the source of most great stories and jokes used in the pulpit today. Once they are in the public domain, it is amazing how quickly they do the rounds and, in the process, become anonymous. So, if you came up with anything that's printed here, thank you!

Finally, we would like to say a special thank you to the Prayer Book Society. It was their complaint about one of the items in *A Box of Delights* that resulted in some welcome, free publicity for that volume in the national press. As a result of their intervention, the sales figures were greatly improved. While we are sorry for any offence caused, we are extremely grateful for their kind help.

Introduction

In this volume we are happy to pass on to you what we have received from many sources: some great illustrations to spice up your talks.

There is no doubt that the ability to illustrate a truth in a humorous, poignant and vivid way is an enormous asset to any speaker. It is of special importance to the Christian communicator. Whatever context you are in — a church, club, dinner party, pub, restaurant, school, or whatever — the ability to express profound, eternal truths in a simple yet vivid way is essential. This was the gift Jesus had, and it is one of the main reasons why he is regarded as the greatest communicator in the whole of history.

Of course, some of the best illustrations come from our own lives. A few Sundays ago one of our staff team here at St Andrews was preaching at a service where four adults had been baptized by total immersion. Greg was speaking about baptism from Romans chapter six and talking about being set free to become a brand new person in Christ Jesus. He was encouraging people to see baptism as an outward sign of that inward transformation. He was also encouraging the newly baptized to think, speak and behave out of the new rather than the old.

The moment everyone in the church understood the point was when my colleague used a simple illustration. For two years he had been senior chaplain of a young offenders' institution. During that time he had worked out of an office in the prison. Obviously, he was not allowed to keep anything in his office or his desk that could have been stolen and then used either as a weapon or as a means of escape. This meant that he had not been allowed to use scissors for two years. Imagine trying to tear everything by hand during that period!

After those two years Greg moved to a Bible college, which is where he has been teaching part time since. He talked about the first few months at his desk in his office in the Bible college, confessing that he was now allowed scissors but that he couldn't get out of the habit of tearing everything by hand. He had grown so used to one way of doing things in a prison that he could not adapt to the new context of a Bible college.

Greg then drove the point home. He underlined the fact that many Christians behave exactly like he did. We have been set free from prison but we behave as if we still live there. Through rebirth we have been set free from the old way of life, with all its restrictions, and have entered into the new life of God's liberty. Let's not believe and behave as if we're still behind bars.

There were scores of non-Christians present who were able to engage with the speaker's message. There were hundreds of young people, teens and twenty-somethings, who got the point. Through an apt illustration from the down-to-earth life of the speaker, truth became incarnate again that night.

Illustrations from everyday life are therefore of great benefit to the preacher.

Obviously these need to be used sparingly, wisely and with humility. We do not preach ourselves, after all, we preach Jesus Christ as Lord (2 Corinthians 4:5). However, we are convinced that Jesus was a great illustrator, and that his illustrations were drawn from what he saw and experienced. As he observed everyday life, he was empowered by the Holy Spirit to hear echoes of the heavenly in the ordinariness of the earthly. It is this parabolic way of thinking which we need so urgently to recapture today.

So we hope you enjoy and benefit from this new treasury of resources. May the Holy Spirit enable you to use these well, and to find yours too, both in your own story, and in the stories of others.

Mark Stibbe and J. John, April 2002

A

Action

> Did is a word of achievement
> Won't is a word of retreat
> Might is a word of bereavement
> Can't is a word of defeat
> Ought is a word of duty
> Try is a word for each hour
> Will is a word of beauty
> Can is a word of power.

"God save us from hotheads who lead us to act foolishly and from cold feet that would keep us from acting at all."
Peter Marshall

"Even if you're on the right track, you'll get run over if you just sit there."
Will Rogers

"It is by acts and not by ideas that people live."
Anatole France

It isn't the number of people employed in a business that makes it successful, it's the number working.

Age

A couple was invited to dinner by their elderly neighbours. The old gentleman endearingly preceded every request to his wife with "Honey", "Darling", "Sweetheart", "Pumpkin", etc.

The neighbors were impressed since the couple had been married almost 70 years.

While the wife was off in the kitchen, the neighbour said to the gentleman, "I think it's wonderful that after all the years you've been married, you still refer to your wife in those terms."

The elderly husband hung his head. "Actually, I forgot the old lady's name about ten years ago."

Arnold and Betty were cleaning out the attic one day when he came across a ticket from the local shoe repair shop. The date stamped on the ticket showed it was over 11 years old. They both laughed and tried to remember which of them might have forgotten to pick up a pair of shoes over a decade ago.

"Do you think the shoes will still be in the shop?" Arnold asked.

"Not very likely," Betty said.

"It's worth a try," Arnold said, pocketing the ticket.

He went downstairs, hopped into the car, and drove to the store. With a straight face, he handed the ticket to the man behind the counter. With a face just as straight, the man said, "Just a minute. I'll have to look for these."

He disappeared into a dark corner at the back of the shop. Two minutes later the man called out, "Here they are!"

"No kidding?" Arnold called back. "That's terrific! Who would have thought they'd still be here after all this time!"

The man came back to the counter, empty-handed.

"They'll be ready on Thursday," he said calmly.

Two elderly couples were chatting together. One of the men asked the other, "Fred, how was the visit to the memory clinic last month?"

"Outstanding. They taught us some of the latest techniques for remembering things. It was great."

"What was the name of this clinic?" asked the other man.

Fred's mind went blank. Then he smiled and asked, "What do you call that flower with the long stem and thorns?"

"A rose?"

"Yes!"

He turned to his wife: "Rose, what was the name of that memory clinic?"

You have reached middle age when all you exercise is caution.

How do I know that my youth is all spent?
Well my "get up and go" has got up and went
But I don't really mind when I think with a grin
Of all the grand places my get has been in
Old age is golden, I've heard it said
But sometimes I wonder as I get into bed
With my rings in a drawer my teeth in a cup
My eyes on the table for when I get up
Ere sleep comes to me I say to myself
Is there anything else I should lay on the shelf?
When I was young my slippers were red
I could kick my heels right over my head
When I grew older my slippers were blue
But still I could dance the whole night through
Now I'm old my slippers are black
I walk to the store and puff my way back
I get up each morning and gather my wits
Pick up the paper and read the "obits"
If my name is still missing
I know I'm not dead
So I have a good breakfast
And go back to bed!

Anon.

We do not stop playing because we grow old;
we grow old because we stop playing.

A little old couple walked slowly into McDonalds one cold winter evening. They looked out of place among the young families and young couples eating there that night.

Some of the customers looked admiringly at them. You could tell what the admirers were thinking. "Look, there is a couple who has been through a lot together, probably for 60 years or more!"

The little old man walked right up to the cash register, placed his order with no hesitation and then paid for their meal. The couple took a table near the back wall and started taking food off the tray. There was one hamburger, one order of French fries and one drink.

The little old man unwrapped the plain hamburger and carefully cut it in half. He placed one half in front of his wife. Then he carefully counted out the French fries, divided them in two piles and neatly placed one pile in front of his wife.

He took a sip of the drink, his wife took a sip and then set the cup down between them.

As the man began to eat his few bites of hamburger the crowd began to get restless. Again you could tell what they were thinking. "That poor old couple. All they can afford is one meal for the two of them."

As the man began to eat his French fries one young man stood and came over to the old couple's table. He politely offered to buy another meal for the old couple. The old man replied that they were just fine. They were used to sharing everything.

Then the crowd noticed that the little old lady hadn't eaten a bite. She just sat there watching her husband eat, occasionally taking turns sipping the drink. Again the young man came over and begged them to let him buy them something to eat. This time the lady explained that no, they were used to sharing everything.

As the little old man finished eating and began wiping his face neatly with a napkin the young man could stand it no longer. Again he came over to their table and offered to buy some food. After being politely refused again he finally asked a question of the little old lady.

"Ma'am, why aren't you eating? You said that you share everything. What is it that you are waiting for?"

She answered… "the teeth".

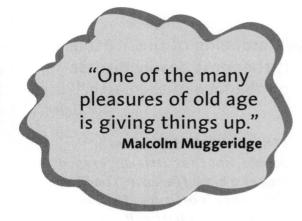

"One of the many pleasures of old age is giving things up."
Malcolm Muggeridge

At 20, we don't care what the world thinks of us; at 30, we worry about what it's thinking of us; at 40 we discover it isn't thinking about us at all!

"You're not as young as you used to be, but you're not as old as you're going to be. So watch it!"

Irish proverb

God grant me the senility to forget the people that I never liked anyway and the good fortune to run into the ones that I do, and the eyesight to tell the difference.

Do not resist growing old — many are denied the privilege.

Arrogance

A young and foolish pilot wanted to sound cool and show who was boss on the aviation frequencies. So, the first time he approached an airfield at night, instead of making his official request to the tower, he said: "Guess who?"

The controller switched the field lights off and replied: "Guess where!"

Attitude

Attitude is the mind's paintbrush. It can color any situation.

"Hardening of the attitudes is the most deadly disease on the face of the earth."

Zig Ziglar

"There is little difference in people, but that little difference makes a big difference. The little difference is attitude. The big difference is whether it is positive or negative."

Clement Stone

It is not the outlook but the uplook that counts.

"Don't bother to give God instructions; just report for duty."

Corrie Ten Boom

It isn't hard to make a mountain out of a molehill. Just add a little dirt.

"Always imitate the behavior of the winners when you lose."

George Meredith

"We lost because we told ourselves we lost."

Leo Tolstoy

The world is full of cactus, but we don't have to sit on it.

There's no danger of developing eyestrain from looking at the bright side of things.

You can often change things if you change attitude.

> "We who lived in concentration camps can remember the men who walked through the huts comforting others, giving away their last piece of bread. They may have been few in number, but they offer sufficient proof that everything can be taken from a man but one thing: the last of the human freedoms — to choose one's attitude in any given set of circumstances."
>
> **Victor Frankl**

Authority

This is the transcript of a genuine radio conversation between a US naval ship and Canadian authorities off the coast of Newfoundland in October 1995:

Americans: *Please divert your course 15 degrees north to avoid a collision.*

Canadians: *Recommend YOU divert YOUR course 15 degrees to the south to avoid a collision.*

Americans: *This is the captain of the US navy ship. I say again, divert YOUR course.*

Canadians: *No, I say again, divert YOUR course.*

Americans: *This is the aircraft carrier USS Lincoln, the second largest ship in the US Atlantic fleet. We are accompanied by three destroyers, three cruisers, and numerous support vessels. I demand that you change your course 15 degrees north, that's ONE FIVE degrees north, or counter-measures will be undertaken to ensure the safety of the ship.*

Canadians: *We're a lighthouse. Your call...*

B

Bible

"I'm not supposed to give these away," the young man said, handing me a display Bible, "but I sense you should have this." I shrugged and absently tucked it away. We had a Bible at home. I'd only stopped by the Gideons' table because nothing else at the Iowa State Fair was set up.

A few days later I was walking to town when a car pulled up beside me. "Get in," the driver snarled, pointing a gun at me. I did as he said. Soon he pulled over, grabbed me and tried to force me down on the seat. I struggled with all my strength. Finally he ordered me out of the car.

Before both my feet were on the ground, I heard a shot and felt a sharp pain in my side. I collapsed, and the man came around the car. He picked up my purse, took out my wallet then threw the purse on my head and shot it. I felt a dreadful impact. Still conscious, I lay silent, hoping he would think I was dead. I heard the car drive away, and I stumbled to a nearby farmhouse. A woman called for help, and soon the police were closing in on the drug-crazed driver based on the description I'd given them.

At the hospital, just before I went into surgery to remove the bullet in my side, my sister came to see me. "Do you know what saved your life, Mavis?" she asked.

She handed me the Bible that had been in my purse. A bullet was lodged inside, its tip stopping exactly at Psalm 37:14–15: "The wicked draw the sword, and bend the bow...to slay those whose ways are upright. But their swords will pierce their own hearts, and their bows will be broken."

(A true story)

Harold Hill, President of the Curtis Engine Company in Baltimore, Maryland, and a consultant in the US space program, relates the following development.

"Our astronauts and space scientists were checking the position of the sun, moon, and planets out in space where they would be 100 years and 1,000 years from now. We have to know this so we won't send a satellite up and have it bump into something later on its orbits. We have to lay out the orbits in terms of the life of the satellite, and where the planets will be, so the whole thing will not bog down.

"They ran the computer measurement back and forth over the centuries. The computer suddenly stopped and put up a red signal, which meant that there was something wrong either with the information fed into it or with the results as compared to the standards. They called in the service department to check it out, and they found there is a day missing in space in elapsed time. They scratched their heads and tore their hair. There was no answer.

"Finally, a Christian man on the team said, 'You know, one time I was in Sunday School and they talked about the sun standing still.' While they didn't believe him, they didn't have an answer either, so they said, 'Show us'. He got a Bible and went back to the book of Joshua where they found a pretty ridiculous statement for any one with 'common sense'. There they found the Lord saying to Joshua, 'Do not fear them, for I have delivered them into your hand; not a man of them shall stand before thee.' Joshua was concerned because he was surrounded by the enemy and if darkness fell they would overpower them. So Joshua asked the Lord to make the sun stand still. That's right — 'The sun stood still and the moon stayed — and hasted not to go down about a whole day!' The astronauts and scientists said, 'There is the missing day!'

"They checked the

computers going back to the time it was written and found it was close but not close enough. The elapsed time that was missing back in Joshua's day was 23 hours and 20 minutes — not a whole day. They read the Bible and there it was: 'about (approximately) a full day'. These little words in the Bible are important but they were still in trouble because if you cannot account for 40 minutes you'll still be in trouble 1,000 years from now. Forty minutes had to be found because it can be multiplied many times over in orbits.

"As the Christian employee thought about it, he remembered somewhere in the Bible where it said the sun went BACKWARDS. The scientists told him he was out of his mind, but they got out the Book and read these words in 2 Kings: 'Hezekiah, on his death-bed, was visited by the prophet Isaiah who told him that he was not going to die. Hezekiah asked for a sign as proof. Isaiah said "Shall the shadow go forward 10 degrees?" Hezekiah said "It is an easy thing for the shadow to go down 10 degrees; no, but let the shadow go backwards 10 degrees…" Isaiah spoke to the Lord and the Lord brought the shadow ten degrees BACKWARD!'

"Ten degrees is exactly 40 minutes! Twenty-three hours and 20 minutes in Joshua, plus 40 minutes in Second Kings make the missing day in the universe!

(References: Joshua 10:8, 12, 13 and 2 Kings 20:9–11, New King James Version, Thomas Nelson 1982)

Emergency Phone Numbers:

When in sorrow...	*call John 14*
When others fail you...	*call Psalm 27*
If you want to be fruitful...	*call John 15*
When you have sinned...	*call Psalm 51*
When you worry...	*call Matthew 6:19–34*
When you are in danger...	*call Psalm 91*
When God seems far away...	*call Psalm 139*
When your faith needs stirring...	*call Hebrews 11*
When you are lonely and fearful...	*call Psalm 23*
When you grow bitter and critical...	*call 1 Corinthians 13*
For Paul's secret to happiness...	*call Colossians 3:12–17*
For understanding of Christianity...	*call 2 Corinthians 5:15–19*
When you feel down and out...	*call Romans 8:31*
When you want peace and rest...	*call Matthew 11:25–30*
When the world seems bigger than God...	*call Psalm 90*
When you want Christian assurance...	*call Romans 8:1–30*
When you leave home for work or travel...	*call Psalm 121*
When your prayers grow narrow or selfish...	*call Psalm 67*
For a great invention/opportunity...	*call Isaiah 55*
When you want courage for a task...	*call Joshua 1*
For how to get along with your fellow man...	*call Romans 12*
When you think of investments and returns...	*call Mark 10*
If you are depressed...	*call Psalm 27*
If your pocketbook/wallet is empty...	*call Psalm 37*
If you are losing confidence in people...	*call 1 Corinthians 13*
If people seem unkind...	*call John 15*
If you are discouraged about your work...	*call Psalm 126*
If you find the world growing small and yourself great...	*call Psalm 19*

Alternative numbers:

For dealing with fear...	*call Psalm 34:7*
For security...	*call Psalm 121:3*
For assurance...	*call Mark 8:35*
For reassurance...	*call Psalm 145:18*

NOTE: ALL LINES TO HEAVEN ARE OPEN 24 HOURS A DAY!

Bible, in 50 words

God made
Adam bit
Noah arked
Abraham split
Joseph ruled
Jacob fooled
Bush talked
Moses balked
Pharaoh plagued
People walked
Sea divided
Tablets guided
Promise landed
Saul freaked
David peeked
Prophets warned
Jesus born
God walked
Love talked
Anger crucified
Hope died
Love rose
Spirit flamed
Word spread
God remained.

Theme Songs for Bible Characters

Noah:	"Raindrops Keep Falling on My Head"
Adam and Eve:	"Strangers in Paradise"
Lazarus:	"The Second Time Around"
Esther:	"I Feel Pretty"
Job:	"I've Got a Right to Sing the Blues"
Moses:	"The Wanderer"
Jezebel:	"The Lady is a Tramp"
Samson:	"Hair"
Salome:	"I Could Have Danced All Night"
Daniel:	"The Lion Sleeps Tonight"
Joshua:	"Good Vibrations"
Peter:	"I'm Sorry"
Esau:	"Born To Be Wild"
Jeremiah:	"Take This Job and Shove It"
Shadrach, Meshach, and Abednego:	"Great Balls of Fire!"
The Three Kings:	"When You Wish Upon a Star"
Jonah:	"Got a Whale of a Tale"
Elijah:	"Up, Up, and Away"
Methuselah:	"Stayin' Alive"
Nebuchadnezzar:	"Crazy"

Bible (trivia quiz)

Q.   Who was the greatest financier in the Bible?
A.   Noah: he was floating his stock while everyone else was in liquidation.

Q.   Who was the greatest female financier in the Bible?
A.   Pharaoh's daughter: she went down to the bank of the Nile and drew out a little prophet.

Q.   What kind of man was Boaz before he got married?
A.   Ruth-less.

Q.   What kind of motor vehicles are in the Bible?
A.   Jehovah drove Adam and Eve out of the Garden in a Fury.
     David's Triumph was heard throughout the land.
     Honda…because the apostles were all in one Accord.
     2 Corinthians 4:8 describes going out to do the Lord's work in a Volkswagen Beetle: "We are pressed in every way, but not cramped beyond movement."

Q.   Who was the greatest comedian in the Bible?
A.   Samson: he brought the house down.

Q.   Which servant of Jehovah was the most flagrant lawbreaker in the Bible?
A.   Moses, because he broke all ten commandments at once.

Q.   Where is the first tennis match mentioned in the Bible?
A.   When Joseph served in Pharaoh's court.

Q.   Which Bible character had no parents?
A.   Joshua, son of Nun.

Q.   Why didn't Noah go fishing?
A.   He only had two worms!

Billboards

The following have been used in the USA and were designed to be seen by car drivers:

Let's meet at my house Sunday before the game — God

C'mon over and bring the kids — God

What part of "Thou Shalt Not…" didn't you understand? — God

We need to talk — God

Keep using my name in vain, I'll make rush hour longer — God

Loved the wedding, invite me to the marriage — God

That "Love Thy Neighbor" thing… I meant it — God

I love you and you and you and you and… — God

Will the road you're on get you to my place? — God

My way is the highway — God

Need directions? — God

You think it's hot here? — God

Don't make me come down there — God

C

Change

Scientists have come up with a term to describe organisms that are not constantly changing: it's "DEAD".

It was all so different before everything changed.

Nostalgia isn't what it used to be.

"No one likes a change except a wet baby."
Noel Coward

"It is good for people to change their minds occasionally in order to keep them clean."
Luther Burbank

Many people hate any change that doesn't jingle in their pocket.

Change is inevitable, except from a vending machine.

"Never doubt the power of a small group of committed people to change the world. That's about the only way it has ever happened in the past." **Margaret Mead, anthropologist**

The Canada and US standard railroad gauge (distance between the rails) is 4 feet, 8.5 inches. That's an exceedingly odd number.

Why was that gauge used? Because that's the way they built them in England, and the US railroads were built by English expatriates.

Why did the English build them like that? Because the first rail lines were built by the same people who built the pre-railroad tramways, and that's the gauge they used.

Why did "they" use that gauge then? Because the people who built the tramways used the same jigs and tools that they used for building wagons, which used that wheel spacing.

Okay! Why did the wagons have that particular odd wheel spacing?

Well, if they tried to use any other spacing, the wagon wheels would break on some of the old long-distance roads in England, because that's the spacing of the wheel ruts. So who built those old rutted roads?

The first long-distance roads in Europe (and England) were built by Imperial Rome for its legions. The roads have been used ever since. And the ruts in the roads? The initial ruts, which everyone else had to match for fear of destroying their wagon wheels, were first formed by Roman war chariots.

Since the chariots were made for (or by) Imperial Rome, they were all alike in the matter of wheel spacing. The United States standard railroad gauge of 4 feet, 8.5 inches derives from the original specification for an Imperial Roman war chariot.

"When you're through changing, you're through."
Bruce Barton

Children

At the beach a child found a seagull lying dead in the sand by the shore.

"Mummy, what happened to him?" the little boy asked.

"He died and went to Heaven," the mother replied.

The child thought for a moment and then said, "And God threw him back down?"

A person is never so tall as when they stoop to help a child.

The child who is being raised strictly by the book is probably a first edition.

A couple had two little boys, ages eight and ten, who were excessively mischievous. The two were always getting into trouble and their parents could be assured that if any mischief occurred in their town their two young sons were in some way involved. The parents were at their wits' end as to what to do about their sons' behavior.

The mother had heard that a clergyman in town had been successful in disciplining children in the past, so she asked her husband if he thought they should send the boys to speak with the clergyman. The husband said, "We might as well. We need to do something before I really lose my temper!" The clergyman agreed to speak with the boys, but asked to see them individually.

The eight-year-old went to meet with him first. The clergyman sat the boy down and asked him sternly, "Where is God?"

The boy made no response, so the clergyman repeated the question in an even sterner tone, "Where is God?"

Again the boy made no attempt to answer. So the clergyman raised his voice even more and shook his finger in the boy's face, "WHERE IS GOD?"

At that the boy bolted from the room and ran straight home, slamming himself in the closet.

His older brother followed him into the closet and said, "What happened?"

The younger brother replied, "We are in BIG trouble this time. God is missing and they think we did it."

A little boy was attending his first wedding. After the service, his cousin asked him, "How many women can a man marry?"

"Sixteen," the boy responded.

His cousin was amazed that he knew the answer so quickly. "How do you know that?"

"Easy," the little boy said. "All you have to do is add it up, like the Bishop said: 4 better, 4 worse, 4 richer, 4 poorer."

A Sunday School teacher asked her class to draw a picture of their favorite Old Testament story, and as she moved around the class, she saw there were many wonderful drawings being done. Then she came across Johnny, who had drawn an old man driving a car. In the back seat were two passengers, both apparently naked.

"It's a lovely picture," said the teacher, "but which story does it tell?"

Johnny seemed surprised at the question. "Doesn't it say in the Bible that God drove Adam and Eve out of the Garden of Eden?"

After a church service on Sunday morning, a young boy suddenly announced to his mother, "Mum, I've decided to become a minister when I grow up."

"That's okay with us, but what made you decide that?"

"Well," said the little boy, "I have to go to church on Sunday anyway, and I figure it will be more fun to stand up and yell, than to sit and listen."

After the dedication of his baby brother in church, a little boy sobbed all the way home in the back seat of the car. His father asked him three times what was wrong. Finally, the boy replied, "That preacher said he wanted us brought up in a Christian home, and I want to stay with you guys!"

A boy was watching his father, a pastor, write a sermon. "How do you know what to say?" he asked.

"Why, God tells me."

"Then why do you keep crossing things out?"

A little boy opened the big old family Bible with fascination, peering at the ancient pages as he turned them.

Then something fell out of the Bible and he picked up and looked at it closely. It was an old leaf from a tree that had been pressed in between pages.

"Mum, look what I found!" the boy called out.

"What have you got there, dear?" his mother asked.

With astonishment in his voice the young boy answered: "I think it's Adam's suit!"

If a child lives with criticism, he learns to condemn.
If a child lives with hostility, she learns to fight.
If a child lives with ridicule, he learns to be shy.
If a child lives with shame, she learns to feel guilty.
If a child lives with tolerance, he learns to be patient.
If a child lives with encouragement, she learns confidence.
If a child lives with praise, he learns to appreciate.
If a child lives with fairness, she learns justice.
If a child lives with security, he learns to have faith.
If a child lives with approval, she learns to like herself.
If a child lives with acceptance and friendship,
he learns to find love in the world.

Dorothy Law Nolte

Choices

God provides the nuts, but he does not crack them.

"You are free to choose, but the choices you make today will determine what you will have, be, and do in the tomorrows of your life."

Anon

Christianity

"People think it's ironic that Alice Cooper, this rock'n'roll rebel, is a Christian. But it's the most rebellious thing I've ever done. Drinking beer is easy. Trashing your hotel room is easy. But being a Christian — that's a tough call. That's real rebellion."

Christmas

REASONS WHY SANTA CLAUS HAS TO BE A WOMAN!

- Men can't pack a bag.
- Men would rather be dead than caught wearing red velvet.
- Men don't answer their mail.
- Men aren't interested in stockings unless somebody's wearing them.
- Men don't think about buying gifts till Christmas Eve, when it's too late.
- Men refuse to stop and ask for directions when they get lost.
- Finally, being responsible for Christmas would require a commitment.

There once was a man in Russia whose name was Rudolph the Red. He was standing in his house one day with his wife. He looked out the window and saw something happening. He said to his wife, "Look darling. It's raining." She, being the obstinate type, responded, "I don't think so, dear. I think it's snowing." But Rudolph knew better. So he said to his wife, "Let's step outside and we'll find out." Lo and behold, they stepped outside and discovered it was in fact rain. And Rudolph turned to his wife and replied, "I knew it was raining. Rudolph the Red knows rain, dear!"

> *"What if the three wise men had been three wise women? Well, they would have asked for directions and arrived on time, helped deliver the baby, cleaned the stable, brought a casserole and given the child much more practical gifts."*
> **Susan Perlman**

"And there were in the country children keeping watch over their stockings by the fireplace. And lo! Santa Claus came upon them; and they were so afraid. And Santa said unto them: 'Fear not, for behold I bring you good tidings of great joy which will be to all people who can afford them. For unto you will be given great feasts of turkey, stuffing and pudding and many presents; and this shall be a sign unto you, ye shall find the presents, wrapped in bright paper, lying beneath a tree adorned with tinsel, colored balls and lights. And suddenly there will be with you a multitude of relatives and friends, praising you and saying, 'Thank you so much, it was just what I wanted.' And it shall come to pass as the friends and relatives have gone away into their own homes, the parents shall say to one another, 'What a mess to clear up! I'm tired, let's go to bed and pick it up tomorrow. Thank goodness, Christmas only comes once a year!'"

A stingy man went Christmas shopping, but everything he saw was too expensive except a £50 vase that was on sale for £2, because the handle had been broken off.

He bought it and had the sales assistant mail it so that his friend would think that he had paid £50 for it, and that it had been broken in the mail.

A week after Christmas he received a thank you note from his friend. "Thank you for the lovely vase," his letter read. "It was so nice of you to wrap each piece separately."

A four-year-old boy was asked to give thanks before Christmas dinner. The family members bowed their heads in expectation. He began his prayer, thanked God for all his friends, naming them one by one. Then he thanks God for Mummy, Daddy, brother, sister, Grandma, Grandpa, and all his aunts and uncles. Then he began to thank God for the food.

He gave thanks for the turkey, the stuffing, the gravy, the cranberry sauce, the mince pies, the Christmas pudding, even the brandy butter.

Then he paused, and everyone waited — and waited. After a long silence, the young boy looked up at his mother and asked, "If I thank God for the sprouts, won't he know that I'm lying?"

During the winter of 1926, Thelma Goldstein treated herself to her first real vacation in Florida.

Being unfamiliar with the area, she wandered into a restricted hotel in North Miami. "Excuse me," she said to the manager. "My name is Mrs Goldstein, and I'd like a small room for two weeks."

"I'm awfully sorry," he replied, "but all of our rooms are occupied."

Just as he said that, a man came down and checked out. "What luck," said Mrs Goldstein. "Now there's a room."

"Not so fast, Madam. I'm sorry, but this hotel is restricted. No Jews allowed."

"Jewish? Who's Jewish? I happen to be Catholic."

"I find that hard to believe. Let me ask you, who was the Son of God?"

"Jesus, Son of Mary."

"Where was he born?"

"In a stable."

"And why was he born in a stable?"

"Because a schmuck like you wouldn't let a Jew rent a room in his hotel!"

Can you decipher the REAL titles of these exaggerated titles of very familiar Christmas tunes? Don't peek now — but if you need help, find the answers below.

1. From dark 'til dawn, soundless and sanctimonious
2. Celestial messengers from splendid empires
3. In a distant bovine diner
4. Universal elation
5. Ornament the enclosure with large sprigs of berry-bearing evergreen
6. O miniature Nazarene village
7. May Jehovah grant unto you hilarious males retirement
8. Those of you who are true, come here!
9. Are you detecting the same aural sensations as I am?
10. The diminutive male of less than adult age who plays a percussion instrument
11. Primary Yuletide
12. Heavenly cherubs announcing in song — listen!

Answers: 1. Silent Night; 2. Angels We Have Heard on High; 3. Away in a Manger; 4. Joy to the World; 5. Deck the Halls with Boughs of Holly; 6. O Little Town of Bethlehem; 7. God Rest You Merry, Gentlemen; 8. O Come, All Ye Faithful; 9. Do You Hear What I Hear?; 10. Little Drummer Boy; 11. The First Noel; 12. Hark, the Herald Angels Sing

Church

A young boy came to Sunday School late. His teacher knew that he was usually very punctual and asked him if anything was wrong. The boy replied no, that he was going fishing but his dad told him that he needed to go to church.

The teacher was very impressed and asked the boy if his dad had explained to him why it was more important to go to church than to go fishing.

To which the boy replied, yes he did, dad said he didn't have enough bait for both of us.

A legend recounts the return of Jesus to heaven after His time on earth. He returned bearing the marks of His earthly pilgrimage with its cruel cross and shameful death.

The Angel Gabriel approached Him and said, "Master you must have suffered terribly for people down there."

"I did," said Jesus.

"And," continued Gabriel, "do they now know all about how you loved them and what you did for them?"

"Oh no," said Jesus. "Not yet. Right now, only a handful of people in Israel know."

Gabriel was perplexed. "Then what have you done," he asked, "to let all people know about your love for them?"

"Well, I have asked Peter, James, John and a few others to tell people about Me. Those who are told will in turn tell others and the gospel will be spread to the farthest reaches of the globe. Ultimately all of humankind will hear about Me and what I have done on their behalf."

Gabriel frowned and looked skeptical. He knew people weren't dependable. "Yes," he said, "but what if Peter, James and John grow weary? What if the people who come after them forget? And what if, way down in the 20th and 21st centuries, people get too busy to bother telling others about you; haven't you made any other plans?"

"No, I have made no other plans, Gabriel," Jesus answered. "I'm counting on them."

Cinema

Things You Would Never Have Known Without Movies:

The ventilation system of any building is the perfect hiding place. No one will ever think of looking for you in there and you can travel to every other part of the building without difficulty.

Should you wish to pass yourself off as a German officer, it will not be necessary to speak the language. A German accent will do.

A man will show no pain while taking the most ferocious beating but will wince when a woman tries to clean his wounds.

Kitchens don't have light switches. When entering a kitchen at night, you should open the fridge door and use that light instead.

If you find yourself caught up in a misunderstanding that could be cleared up quickly with a simple explanation, for goodness' sake, keep your mouth shut.

All bombs are fitted with electronic timing devices with large red readouts so you know exactly when they're going to go off.

One man shooting at 20 men has a better chance of killing them than 20 men firing at one man.

Creepy music coming from a cemetery should always be investigated more closely.

When being fired at by Germans, hide in a river — or even a bath. German bullets are unable to penetrate water.

When they are all alone, all foreigners prefer to speak English to each other.

Action heroes never face charges for manslaughter or criminal damage despite laying waste entire cities by their actions.

An electric fence powerful enough to kill a dinosaur will cause no lasting damage to an eight-year-old child.

Honest and hard-working policemen are traditionally gunned down three days before their retirement.

The more a man and a woman seem to hate each other, the more likely they will fall in love.

Commandments

1. You shall not worry for worry is the most unproductive of all human activities.

2. You shall not be fearful, for most of the things we fear never come to pass.

3. You shall not carry grudges, for they are the heaviest of all life's burdens.

4. You shall face each day as it comes. You can only handle one day at a time anyway.

5. You shall not take problems to bed with you, for they make very poor bedfellows.

6. You shall not borrow other people's problems. They can better care for them than you.

7. You shall not try to relive yesterday for good or ill; it is forever gone. Concentrate on what is happening in your life and be happy now!

8. You shall be a good listener, for only when you listen do you hear ideas different from your own.

9. You shall not become "bogged down" by frustration, for 90% of it is rooted in self-pity and will only interfere with positive action.

10. You shall count your blessings, never overlooking the small ones, for a lot of small blessings add up to a big one.

Commitment

Butt Prints in the Sand

One night I had a wondrous dream,
One set of footprints there was seen,
The footprints of my precious Lord,
But mine were not along the shore.

But then some stranger prints appeared,
And I asked the Lord, "What have we here?
Those prints are large and round and neat,
But Lord, they are too big for feet."

"My child," He said in somber tones,
"For miles I carried you alone.
Challenged you to walk in faith,
But you refused and made me wait.

"You disobeyed, you would not grow,
The walk of faith, you would not know,
So I got tired, I got fed up,
And there I dropped you on your butt.

"Because in life, there comes a time,
When one must fight, and one must climb,
When one must rise and take a stand,
Or leave their butt prints in the sand."

Communication

Making telephone contact with people used to be rather simple. Modern technology has changed all that. Now there is call waiting, answering machines, and electronic operators. You can spend five minutes trying to get past all the interference.

Have you heard about the new psychiatric hotline? When you phone in you get this message:

- If you are obsessive-compulsive, please press 1 repeatedly.
- If you are co-dependent, please ask someone else to press 2.
- If you have multiple personalities, please press 3, 4, 5 and 6.
- If you are paranoid-delusional, we know who you are and what you want. Just stay on the line so that we can trace your call.
- If you are schizophrenic, listen carefully and a little voice will tell you which number to press.
- If you are manic-depressive, it doesn't matter which number you press. No one will answer.

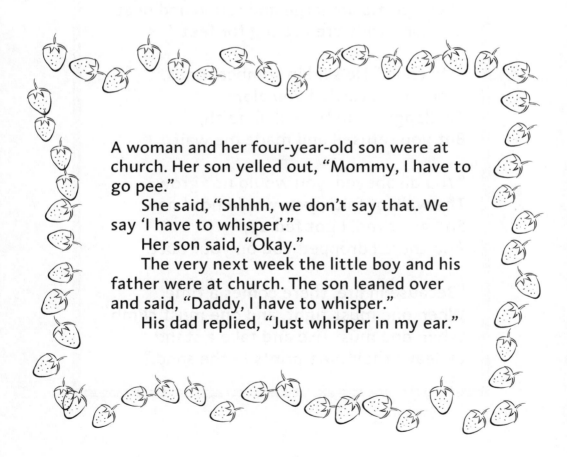

A woman and her four-year-old son were at church. Her son yelled out, "Mommy, I have to go pee."

She said, "Shhhh, we don't say that. We say 'I have to whisper'."

Her son said, "Okay."

The very next week the little boy and his father were at church. The son leaned over and said, "Daddy, I have to whisper."

His dad replied, "Just whisper in my ear."

A member of a certain church, who had previously attended services regularly, stopped going. After a few weeks, the minister decided to visit him. It was a chilly evening. The pastor found the man at home alone, sitting before a blazing fire. Guessing the reason for his pastor's visit, the man welcomed him, led him to a big chair near the fireplace and waited.

The pastor made himself comfortable but said nothing. In the grave silence, he contemplated the play of the flames around the burning logs. After some minutes, the pastor took the fire tongs, carefully picked up a brightly burning ember and placed it to one side of the hearth all on its own. Then he sat back in his chair, still silent.

The host watched all this in quiet fascination. As the lone ember's flame diminished, there was a momentary glow and then its fire was no more. Soon it was cold and dead.

Not a word had been spoken since the initial greeting. Just before the pastor was ready to leave, he picked up the cold, dead ember and placed it back in the middle of the fire. Immediately it began to glow once more with the light and warmth of the burning coals around it.

As the pastor reached the door to leave, his host said, "Thank you so much for your visit and especially for the fiery sermon. I shall be back in church next Sunday."

Knowing that the minister was very fond of cherry brandy, one of the church elders offered to present him with a bottle on one consideration — that the pastor acknowledge receipt of the gift in the church paper.

"Gladly," responded the good man.

When the church magazine came out a few days later, the elder turned at once to the "appreciation" column. There he read: "The minister extends his thanks to Elder Brown for his gift of fruit and for the spirit in which it was given."

Compassion

"We are not put on this earth to see through one another but to see one another through."

Peter de Vries

"Everybody wants to right the world. Nobody wants to help their neighbor."

Henry Miller

Author and lecturer Leo Buscaglia once talked about a contest he had been asked to judge. The purpose of the contest was to find the most caring child. The winner was a four-year-old child whose next door neighbor was an elderly gentleman who had recently lost his wife.

Upon seeing the man cry, the little boy went into the old gentleman's garden, climbed onto his lap, and just sat there.

When his mother asked him what he had said to the neighbor, the little boy said, "Nothing, I just helped him cry."

"There are two key principles for the compassionate person — giving and forgiving."

J. John

A little boy about ten years old was standing before a shoe store on the roadway, barefoot, peering through the window, and shivering with cold. A lady approached the boy and said, "My little fellow, why are you looking so earnestly in that window?" "I was asking God to give me a pair of shoes," was the boy's reply.

The lady took him by the hand and went into the store and asked the assistant to get half a dozen pairs of socks for the boy. She then asked if he could get her a basin of water and a towel.

He quickly brought them to her. She took the little boy to the back part of the store and, removing her gloves, knelt down, washed his little feet, and dried them with a towel. By this time the assistant had returned with the socks.

Placing a pair upon the boy's feet, she bought him a pair of shoes. She tied up the remaining pairs of socks and gave them to him. She patted him on the head and said, "No doubt, my little fellow, you feel more comfortable now?"

As she turned to go, the astonished lad caught her by the hand, and looking up in her face, with tears in his eyes, answered the question with these words: "Are you God's wife?"

Complaints

Here are some actual maintenance complaints generally known as "squawks" or problems submitted recently by pilots to maintenance engineers. (P) is the problem logged by the pilot, and (S) marks the solution and action taken by maintenance engineers.

(P) Target Radar hums
(S) Reprogrammed Target Radar with the words

(P) Test flight OK, except autoland very rough
(S) Autoland not installed on this aircraft

(P) Something loose in cockpit
(S) Something tightened in cockpit

(P) Evidence of leak on right main landing gear
(S) Evidence removed

(P) DME volume unbelievably loud
(S) Volume set to more believable level

(P) Dead bugs on windshield
(S) Live bugs on backorder

(P) Friction locks cause throttle levers to stick
(S) That's what they're there for

(P) Number three engine missing
(S) Engine found on right wing after brief search

"Complaint is the largest tribute that Heaven receives."
Jonathan Swift

Commitment

Letter of Commitment from a church member in the USA:

I think every person ought to be excused for the following reasons and the number of times indicated:

Christmas (Sunday before or after)
New Year (Party lasted too long)
Easter (Get away for holidays)
July 4 (National holiday)
Labor Day (Need to get away)
Memorial Day (Visit hometown)
School Closing (Kids need break)
School Opens (One last fling)
Family Reunions (Mine and wife's)
Sleep late (Saturday night activities)
Deaths in Family
Anniversary (Second honeymoon)
Sickness (One per family member)
Business Trips (A must)
Vacation (Three weeks)
Bad Weather (Ice, snow, rain, clouds)
Ball games
Unexpected company (Can't walk out)
Time changes (Spring ahead; fall back)
Special on TV (Super Bowl, etc.)

Pastor, that leaves only two Sundays per year. So, you can count on us *to be in church* on the *fourth Sunday in February* and the *third Sunday in August* unless providentially hindered.

Sincerely,

A Faithful Member

Confidence

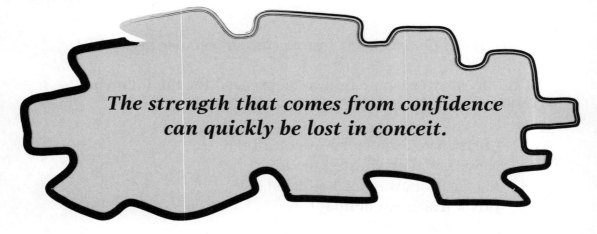

*The strength that comes from confidence
can quickly be lost in conceit.*

Conflict

A friend of mine who is a pastor said this: "Whenever the conflict
gets too much in my church I go and visit the local kennels.
There's a whole group there that's always pleased to see me!"

Co-operation

A magician was working on a cruise ship in the Caribbean. The audience
would be different each week, so the magician allowed himself to do the
same tricks over and over again.

There was only one problem — the captain's parrot saw the shows each
week and began to understand how the magician did every trick. Once he
understood he started shouting in the middle of the show, "Look, it's not the
same hat".

"Look, he is hiding the flowers under the table."

"Hey, why are all the cards the Ace of Spades?"

The magician was furious but couldn't do anything. After all, it WAS the
captain's parrot. One stormy day the ship had an accident and sank. The
magician found himself adrift on a piece of wood in the middle of the
ocean...and the parrot was adrift on this very same piece of wood with him.

They stared at each other with hate, but did not utter a word. This went on
for a day...then another...and then another. After almost three days the
parrot finally says, "OK, I give up. Where the heck is the boat?"

A steering committee is a group of four people trying to park a car.

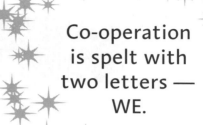

Co-operation is spelt with two letters — WE.

Courage

Police cadets were given a test paper to determine their skills and abilities, which would help senior police officers place them. The paper went like this:

> You are walking down a village street and you hear the honking of a horn. You turn around and see a lorry laden with petrol, charging down a hill out of control. At the crossroads it collides with a milk float and an almighty explosion takes place and the driver of the milk float is hurtled through the plate glass over a wall, whilst the driver of the petrol tanker is trapped in his cab.
>
> You are about to radio for help — when you hear a cry. You rush across the road, picking your way through the broken glass and flaming tarmac. There is the man from the milk float drowning in a canal — he cannot swim.
>
> You are just about to radio for help — when you hear another cry. It is a lady, about to give birth to her child. The explosion has brought on the birth, but she is trapped in her home, the door is stuck and she has no phone. She is in immediate need of medical attention.
>
> You are just about to radio for help — when you hear a noise.
>
> You look behind you and there is a group of men, totally drunk staggering across the road laughing at the whole affair.
>
> In this situation what would you do?

One police cadet wrote: "Remove uniform and mingle with crowd!"

"Courage is the finest of human qualities because it guarantees all the others." **Winston Churchill**

"Courage is resistance to fear, mastery of fear — not absence of fear." **Mark Twain**

"One person with courage is a majority."
Andrew Jackson

There are too many people praying for mountains of difficulty to be removed, when what they really need is the courage to climb them. Courage is being the only one who knows you're afraid.

"The first virtue in a soldier is endurance of fatigue; courage is only the second virtue." **Napoleon Bonaparte**

D

Death

> **C S Lewis** — writing after the death of his wife:
>
> "An odd by-product of my loss is that I am aware of being an embarrassment to everyone I meet, at work, at the club, in the street. I see people as they approach me trying to make up their minds whether they will say something about it or not. I hate it if they do and hate it if they don't. Some avoid it altogether. I like best the well-brought up young men who walk up to me as if I were a dentist, turn very red, get it over and then edge away to the bar as quickly as they decently can. Perhaps the bereaved ought to be isolated in special settlements like lepers."

A minister waited in line to have his car filled with gas just before a long holiday weekend. The attendant worked quickly, but there were many cars ahead of him in front of the service station. Finally, the attendant motioned him toward a vacant pump.

"Reverend," said the young man, "Sorry about the delay. It seems as if everyone waits until the last minute to get ready for a long trip."

The minister chuckled, "I know what you mean. It's the same in my business."

Deeds

> *"If I cannot do great things, I can do small things in a great way."*
> **James F. Clarke**

Denominations

A certain Baptist couple felt it important to own an equally Baptist pet, so they went shopping. At a kennel specializing in this particular breed, they found a dog they liked quite a lot. When they asked the dog to fetch the Bible, he did it in a flash. When instructed to look up Psalm 23, the dog complied equally fast, using his paws with dexterity. They were so impressed that the couple purchased the animal and took him home.

That night the couple had friends over. They were so proud of their new Baptist dog and his great skills that they wanted to show him off. They called the dog and gave him his commands. The friends were impressed, and asked whether the dog was able to do any of the usual dog tricks as well. This stopped the couple cold, as they hadn't thought about "normal" tricks.

"Well," they said, "Let's try it out." Once more they called the dog, and they clearly pronounced the command, "Heel".

As quick as a flash, the dog jumped up, put his paw on the man's forehead, closed his eyes in concentration, and bowed his head!

THEY HAD BEEN DECEIVED... THE DOG WAS A PENTECOSTAL!

(It's a good thing they didn't ask him to "speak".)

Determination

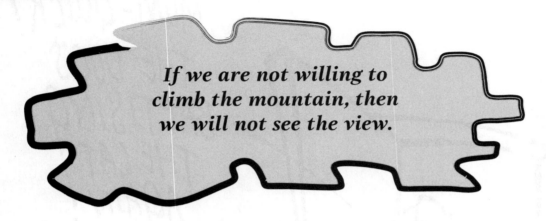

If we are not willing to climb the mountain, then we will not see the view.

Dieting

My diet is my shepherd, I shall be in want,
It makes me jog quietly round and round green pastures,
It leads me to quietly drink water,
And jump on and off the scales.
It guides me to resist all pleasurable food
For my figure's shape.

Even though I walk through the aisles of Sainsbury's
I will buy no Bovril
For you are with me;
Your measuring tape and your calorie counter
They confuse me.

You prepare a table before me
In the presence of the Tellytubbies.
You cover my lettuce with low-fat mayonnaise,
My diet coke overflows.
Surely a rumbling stomach and a feeling of irritability will be with me
All the days of my slimming plan
And I will worry about my weight forever.

Dr Debbie Lovell

Diet (noun): 1. A short period of starvation followed by a gain of five pounds.

I went on a 14-day diet, but all I lost was two weeks.

Brain cells come and brain cells go, but fat cells live forever.

There's a new diet that is all the rage. You can eat all you see of everything you don't like.

Difficulties

A smooth sea never made a skilful mariner.

Dreams

Don't be unhappy if your dreams never come true — just be thankful your nightmares don't.

Some people who think they are dreamers are really just sleepers.

Between tomorrow's dream and yesterday's regret is today's opportunity.

"Hold fast to dreams, for if dreams die, life is a broken-winged bird that cannot fly."
Langston Hughes

"Some people see things as they are and say, 'Why?' I dream things that never were and say, 'Why not?'"
George Bernard Shaw

"In a famous verse in the book of Joel, God promises to pour out his Spirit…when 'your old men shall dream dreams, your young men shall see visions'.

"These ancient and evocative words are surprisingly close to modern reality, according to a survey of a representative sample of 500 people in Britain carried out for Unmissable Ltd, a company which has set out to offer its clients the chance to make their dreams come true. A questionnaire and focus group probed the respondents' dreams and fantasies.

"Among the findings were the ages at which people actually make lists of the things they dream of doing in their lives. Three people in every five have done this. The peak dreaming ages proved to be the very young and the seriously mature. Unsurprisingly, adolescence is the great age for making a wish list, with nearly 70% of under 24s writing down their life's goals… The figures show that as people grow older the wish list is put away, but at 55 it comes out again, with 64% of people in this group keeping a list which is revised, updated and finally used as an agenda for the rest of life."

Celia Brayfield, *The Times*, 6 March 2001

E

Education

One thing we were taught in
school is that double negatives
are a no-no.

Teacher: Name two pronouns.
Student: Who? Me?

*"We are swimming
in information
and starving for
wisdom."*
J.John

"If your plan is for a year, plant rice.
If your plan is for a decade, plant trees.
If your plan is for a lifetime, educate children."
Confucius (551–479 BC)

Comment from a professor to a student:
"I am returning this very good paper to you
because someone has written nonsense all over it
and put your name at the top."

Election

When God was looking for a people to call his own, he went to all the peoples of the world and he asked them what they would do if he became their God and they became his people.

He asked the Greeks, "If I became your God and you became my people, what would you do for me?" And the Greeks said, "Master of the Universe, if you become our God and we become your people, we will create for you the most beautiful works of art and the most profound systems of philosophy the world has ever known. All the people will come and worship you because of your beauty and your wisdom." And God said, "Thank you", and he went on.

And God went to the Romans and he asked, "If I became your God and you became my people, what would you do for me?" The Romans said, "Almighty God, if you become our God and we become your people, we will set your standard at the head of our armies and we will put your banner before the caravans and the fleets of our commercial empire. All people will come and bow down before you because of your power and your might." And God said, "Thank you", and he went on.

And God went to all the peoples of the world and got their offers. Finally he came to a scrawny bunch of nomads in the desert called Hebrews. Now these nomads were shrewd traders and God said to them, "If I became your God and you became my people, what would you do for me?" And the people said, "Lord God, we cannot offer you great works of art or systems of philosophy. It is not within our capability. Nor can we offer you great power or wealth. You can see our poor herds and tents. But if you become our God and we become your people, we will tell the stories of your deeds to our children and they to their children and they to their children to all generations."

And God said, "It's a deal!"

Encouragement

Two men, both seriously ill, occupied the same hospital room. One man was allowed to sit up in bed for an hour each afternoon to help drain the fluid from his lungs. His bed was next to the room's only window. The other man had to spend all his time flat on his back. The men talked for hours on end. They spoke of their wives and families, their homes, their jobs, their military service, where they had been on vacation. And every afternoon when the man in the bed by the window could sit up, he would pass the time by describing to his roommate all the things he could see outside the window.

The man in the other bed began to live for those one-hour periods where his outlook would be broadened and enlivened by all the activity and colour of the world outside. The window overlooked a park with a lovely lake. Ducks and swans played on the water while children sailed their model boats. Young lovers walked arm in arm amidst flowers of every colour of the rainbow. Grand old trees graced the landscape, and a fine view of the city skyline could be seen in the distance.

As the man by the window described all this exquisite detail, the man on the other side of the room would close his eyes and imagine the picturesque scene. One warm afternoon the man by the window described a parade passing by. The other man couldn't hear the band — but he could see it in his mind's eye as the gentleman by the window portrayed it with descriptive words.

Then unexpectedly, a sinister thought entered his mind. Why should the other man alone experience all the pleasures of seeing everything while he himself never got to see anything? It didn't seem fair. At first the man felt ashamed. But as the days passed and he missed seeing more sights, his envy eroded into resentment and soon turned him sour. He began to brood and he found himself unable to sleep. He should be by that window — that thought, and only that thought, now controlled his life.

Late one night as he lay staring at the ceiling, the man by the window began to cough. He was choking on the fluid in his lungs. The other man watched in the dimly lit room as the struggling man by the window groped for the button to call for help. Listening from across the room he never moved, never pushed his own button which would have brought the nurse running in. In less than five minutes the coughing and choking stopped, along with that the sound of breathing. Now there was only silence — deathly silence.

The following morning the day nurse arrived to bring water for their baths. When she found the lifeless body of the man by the window, she was saddened and called the hospital attendants to take it away. As soon as it seemed appropriate, the other man asked if he could be moved next to the window. The nurse was happy to make the switch, and after making sure he was comfortable, she left him alone. Slowly, painfully, he propped himself up on one elbow to take his first look at the world outside. Finally, he would have the joy of seeing it all himself. He strained to slowly turn to look out the window beside the bed. It faced a blank wall.

The man asked the nurse what could have motivated his deceased roommate to describe such wonderful things outside this window. The nurse responded that the man was blind and could not even see the wall. She said, "Perhaps he just wanted to encourage you."

Chuck Swindoll

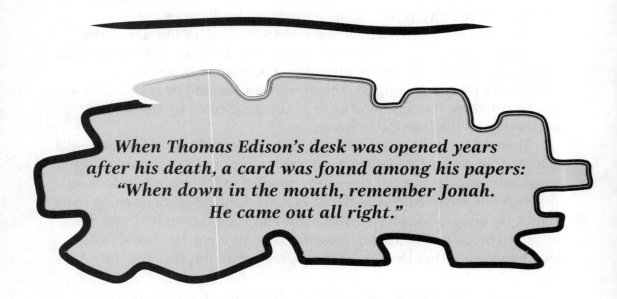

When Thomas Edison's desk was opened years after his death, a card was found among his papers: "When down in the mouth, remember Jonah. He came out all right."

Reach down and lift others up. It's the best exercise you can get.

Expectations

> "The only man who behaved sensibly was my tailor; he took my measurements anew every time he saw me, while all the rest went on with their old measurements and expected them to fit me."
>
> **George Bernard Shaw**

Experience

"Experience is a hard teacher, because she gives the test first and the lesson after."
Vernon Law

Experience is a wonderful thing. It enables you to recognize a mistake when you make it again.

"What we have to learn to do, we learn by doing."
Aristotle

F

Faithfulness

We've heard of the Air Force's ultra-high security, super-secret base in Nevada, known simply as "Area 51". Late one afternoon, the Air Force folks out at Area 51 were very surprised to see a Cessna landing at their "secret" base. They immediately impounded the aircraft and hauled the pilot into an interrogation room.

The pilot explained that he took off from Vegas, got lost, and spotted the Base just as he was about to run out of fuel. The Air Force started a full FBI background check on the pilot and held him overnight during the investigation. By the next day, they were finally convinced that the pilot really was lost and wasn't a spy. They refueled his airplane, gave him a terrifying "you-did-not-see-a-base" briefing, complete with threats of spending the rest of his life in prison, told him Vegas was so many kilometres away on such-and-such a heading, and sent him on his way.

The next day, to the total disbelief of the Air Force, the same Cessna showed up again. Once again, the MPs surrounded the plane, only this time there were two people inside. The same pilot jumped out and said, "Do anything you want to me, but my wife is in the plane and since I can't tell her where I was last night, you have to!"

Families

Sally came home with her new fur coat. When her daughter saw the coat she yelled: "Mum, you should be ashamed of yourself wearing a fur coat! Don't you realize that a poor dumb animal has suffered for that?"

Sally looked at her daughter angrily and shouted: "Don't you dare to talk about your father like that!"

Fatherhood of God

It was the dead of night in Dallas as the doctor walked into the small hospital room of Diana Blessing. That afternoon of 10 March 1991, complications had forced Diana, only 24 weeks pregnant, to undergo an emergency Caesarean to deliver the couple's new daughter, Danae Lu Blessing. At 12 inches long and weighing only one pound and nine ounces, they already knew she was perilously premature. Still, the doctor's soft words dropped like bombs.

"I don't think she's going to make it," he said, as kindly as he could. "There's only a 10 per cent chance she will live through the night, and even then, if by some slim chance she does make it, her future could be a very cruel one."

Numb with disbelief, David and Diana listened as the doctor described the devastating problems Danae would likely face if she survived. She would never walk, she would never talk, she would probably be blind, and she would certainly be prone to other catastrophic conditions from cerebral palsy to complete mental retardation, and on and on. "No! No!" was all Diana could say. She and David, with their five-year-old son Dustin, had long dreamed of the day they would have a daughter to become a family of four. Now, within a matter of hours, that dream was slipping away.

Through the dark hours of morning as Danae held onto life by the thinnest thread, Diana slipped in and out of sleep, growing more and more determined that their tiny daughter would live, and live to be a healthy, happy young girl.

As if willed to live by Diana's determination, Danae clung to life hour after hour, with the help of every medical machine and marvel her miniature body could endure. But as those first days passed, a new agony set in for David and Diana. Because Danae's under-developed nervous system was essentially raw, the lightest kiss or caress only intensified her discomfort, so they couldn't even cradle their tiny baby girl against their chests to offer her the strength of their love. All they could do, as Danae struggled alone beneath the ultraviolet light in the tangle of tubes and wires, was to pray that God would stay close to their precious little girl.

As the weeks went by, she did slowly gain an ounce of weight here and an ounce of strength there. At last, when

Danae was two months old, her parents were able to hold her in their arms for the very first time. And two months later, Danae went home from the hospital, just as her mother had predicted.

Today, Danae is a petite but feisty young lady with glittering grey eyes and an unquenchable zest for life. She shows no signs whatsoever of any mental or physical impairment. Simply, she is everything a girl can be and more — but that happy ending is far from the end of her story.

One blistering afternoon in the summer of 1996 near her home in Irving, Texas, Danae was sitting in her mother's lap at a local park. As always, Danae was chattering non-stop with her mother and several other adults sitting nearby, when she suddenly fell silent. Hugging her arms across her chest, Danae asked, "Do you smell that?"

Smelling the air and detecting the approach of a thunderstorm, Diana replied, "Yes, it smells like rain."

Danae closed her eyes and again asked, "Do you smell that?"

Once again, her mother replied, "Yes, I think we're about to get wet, it smells like rain."

Still caught in the moment, Danae shook her head, patted her thin shoulders with her small hands and loudly announced, "No, it smells like Him. It smells like God when you lay your head on His chest."

Tears blurred Diana's eyes as Danae hopped happily down to play with the other children. Before the rains came, her daughter's words confirmed what Diana and all the members of the extended family had known, at least in their hearts, all along. During those long days and nights of her first two months of life, when her nerves were too sensitive for them to touch her, God was holding Danae on His chest and it is His loving scene that she remembers so well.

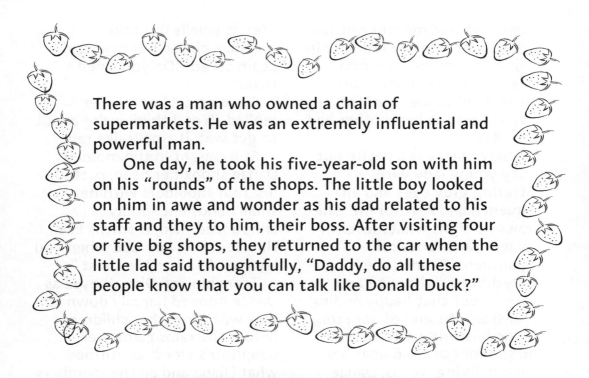

There was a man who owned a chain of supermarkets. He was an extremely influential and powerful man.

One day, he took his five-year-old son with him on his "rounds" of the shops. The little boy looked on him in awe and wonder as his dad related to his staff and they to him, their boss. After visiting four or five big shops, they returned to the car when the little lad said thoughtfully, "Daddy, do all these people know that you can talk like Donald Duck?"

Advice to fathers over 40: keep an open mind and a closed refrigerator.

Greg Norman is one of the most ice-cold golfers on the circuit. He learned this from his father. "I used to see my father, getting off a plane or something, and I'd want to hug him," he said once. "But he'd only shake my hand."

Norman was at the 1996 Masters, golf's most prestigious tournament, when he made these remarks. Norman let a six-shot lead go during the last round, losing to his great rival Nick Faldo.

Faldo hit a 15-foot birdie for the winning shot. He then walked towards Norman, who tried to smile, waiting for the customary handshake. Instead, he found himself in a bear hug embrace from Faldo.

As they held each other, Norman began to weep. Later Norman said, "I wasn't crying because I lost. I've lost a lot of golf tournaments before. I'll lose a lot more. I cried because I'd never felt that from another man before. I've never had a hug like that in my life."

Fiction

In 1898, 14 years before the *Titanic* made her maiden voyage, Morgan Robertson published his book *Futility for the wreck of the Titan*. This was the story of an unsinkable, massive ocean liner which, like the *Titanic*, was on its maiden voyage from Britain to New York with 2,000 on board.

While it was also attempting to cross the Atlantic in record time, it too struck an iceberg and sank. Most on board also perished simply because there was a lack of lifeboats. That was fiction.

On the night of 14 April 1912, the *Titanic* struck an iceberg. Its hull breached, the liner rapidly began taking on water. The waves closed over the *Titanic* at 2:20am ship's time, and the 882-foot ship plunged to the bottom, 13,000 feet below. Of the 2,200 people on board, 1,500 died. The biggest, fastest and grandest ship in the world went to the bottom. It really happened.

Flying

"This is your captain speaking. On behalf of my crew I'd like to welcome you aboard flight 602 from New York to London. We are currently flying at a height of 35,000 feet midway across the Atlanic.

"If you look out of the windows on the starboard side of the aircraft, you will observe that both the starboard engines are on fire.

"If you look out of the windows on the port side, you will observe that the port wing has fallen off.

"If you look down towards the Atlantic ocean, you will see a little yellow life raft with three people in it waving at you.

"That's me, the co-pilot, and one of our flight attendants. This is a recording."

Fulfilment

"Among all my patients in the second half of life, that is, over 35, there has not been one whose problem in the last resort was not that of finding a religious outlook on life. It is safe to say that every one of them fell ill because he had lost that which the living religions of every age have given their followers, and none of them has really been healed who did not regain his religious outlook."

C G Jung, *Modern Man in Search of a Soul*

G

Gambling

There was a Catholic priest who liked to bet on horses. There was one particular horse he favoured and when the horse was running he would always go down to the stables to pray and bless the horse.

A Baptist noticed that when he did this, the horse always won. So he decided to put money on that horse because it kept on winning every time the priest prayed for it.

On a particular day the priest went down to the stables, blessed the horse with water and prayed over it. At once the Baptist went and placed his bet. The horse came last. Feeling very angry, and very poor, the Baptist challenged the priest. "Every time you pray, your horse wins. I saw you pray today, and I bet — and he came last!"

The priest replied, "You know nothing about our Roman Catholic sacraments. You have to know the difference between a blessing, and the last rites."

A racehorse is an animal that can take several thousand people for a ride at the same time.

Giving

There is the story of a minister who got up one Sunday and announced to his congregation: "I have good news and bad news. The good news is, we have enough money to pay for our new building programme. The bad news is, it's still out there in your pockets."

God

We have learned to live with "voice mail" as a necessary part of modern life. But have you wondered what would happen if God decided to install voice mail? Imagine praying and hearing this: "Thank you for calling My Father's House. Please select one of the following options:

> *Press 1 for Requests*
> *Press 2 for Thanksgiving*
> *Press 3 for Complaints*
> *Press 4 for All Other Inquiries"*

What if God used the familiar excuse, "I'm sorry, all our angels are busy helping other saints right now; however, your prayer is important to us and will be answered in the order it was received, so please stay on the line." This might be followed by —

> *If you would like to speak to:*
> *Gabriel, Press 1*
> *Michael, Press 2*
> *For a directory of other angels, Press 3*
> *If you'd like to hear King David sing a psalm while you are holding, press 4*
> *To find out if a loved one has been assigned to Heaven, Press 5, enter his or her social security number, then press the pound key.*
> *(If you get a negative response, try area code 777)*
> *For reservations at "My Father's House" please enter J-O-H-N, followed by 3-1-6. For answers to nagging questions about dinosaurs, the age of the earth and where Noah's Ark is, please wait until you arrive here.*

Alternatively:

> *Our computers show that you have already prayed once today. Please hang up and try again tomorrow so that others may have a chance to get through.*

> *This office is closed for the weekend to observe a religious holiday.*

> *Please pray again Monday after 9:30 am. If you need emergency assistance when this office is closed, contact your local pastor.*

Thank God (today) that He doesn't have voice mail, and that He listens whenever we pray and that will never change!

The will of God will never take you,
where the grace of God cannot keep you,
where the arms of God cannot support you,
where the riches of God cannot supply your needs,
where the power of God cannot endow you.

The will of God will never take you,
where the Spirit of God cannot work through you,
where the wisdom of God cannot teach you,
where the army of God cannot protect you,
where the hands of God cannot mould you.

The will of God will never take you,
where the love of God cannot enfold you,
where the mercies of God cannot sustain you,
where the peace of God cannot calm your fears,
where the authority of God cannot overrule for you.

The will of God will never take you,
where the comfort of God cannot dry your tears,
where the Word of God cannot feed you,
where the miracles of God cannot be done for you,
where the omnipresence of God cannot find you.

Everything happens for a purpose.

We may not see the wisdom of it all now,
but trust and believe in the Lord
that everything is for the best.

Author unknown

Just in case you forgot

If God had a refrigerator, your picture would be on it.
If God had a wallet, your photo would be in it.
He sends you flowers every spring and a sunrise every morning.
When you want to talk, He'll listen.
He could live anywhere in the universe and He chose your heart.

Sherry M Keith

"I find that doing the will of God leaves me with no time for disputing about His plans."
George Macdonald

"There is no situation so chaotic that God cannot, from that situation, create something that is surpassingly good. He did it at the Creation. He did it at the Cross. He is doing it today."
Handley C G Moule

Psalm 23

The Lord is my Shepherd...
> THAT'S RELATIONSHIP!

I shall not want...
> THAT'S SUPPLY!

He maketh me to lie down in green pastures...
> THAT'S REST!

He leadeth me beside still waters...
> THAT'S REFRESHMENT!

He restoreth my soul...
> THAT'S HEALING!

He leadeth me in the paths of righteousness...
> THAT'S GUIDANCE!

For His name sake...
> THAT'S PURPOSE!

Yea, though I walk through the valley of the shadow of death...
> THAT'S CHALLENGE!

I will fear no evil...
> THAT'S ASSURANCE!

For thou art with me...
> THAT'S FAITHFULNESS!

Thy rod and thy staff they comfort me...
> THAT'S SHELTER!

Thou preparest a table before me in the presence of mine enemies...
> THAT'S HOPE!

Thou anointest my head with oil...
> THAT'S CONSECRATION!

My cup runneth over...
> THAT'S ABUNDANCE!

Surely goodness and mercy shall follow me all the days of my life...
> THAT'S BLESSING!

And I will dwell in the house of the Lord...
> THAT'S SECURITY!

Forever...
> THAT'S ETERNITY!

Amen (so be it).

He is the First and Last, the Beginning and the End!
He is the keeper of Creation and the Creator of all!
He is the Architect of the universe and the Lord of history.
He always was, He always is, and He always will be...
Unmoved, Unchanged, Undefeated, Undismayed!
His ways are right,
His word is eternal,
His will is unchanging, and
His worth is inestimable.
He is the King of the Ages
And the Ancient of Days.
He is the leader of leaders
And the ruler of the kings of the earth.

And if that seems impressive to you, try this for size.

His goal is a relationship with ME!
He will never leave me,
Never forsake me,
Never mislead me,
Never forget me,
Never overlook me, and
Never cancel my appointment in His appointment book!

When I fall, He lifts me up!
When I fail, He forgives!
When I am weak, He is strong!
When I am lost, He is the way!
When I am afraid, He is my courage!
When I stumble, He steadies me!
When I am hurt, He heals me!
When I am broken, He mends me!
When I am blind, He leads me!
When I am hungry, He feeds me!
When I face trials, He is with me!
When I face persecution, He shields me!
When I face problems, He comforts me!
When I face loss, He provides for me!
When I face Death, He carries me Home!

He is God, He is faithful.
I am His, and He is mine!

So, if you're wondering why I feel so secure, understand this...
God is in control, I am on His side, and
That means all is well with my soul.

Everyday is a blessing for GOD is!

Grace

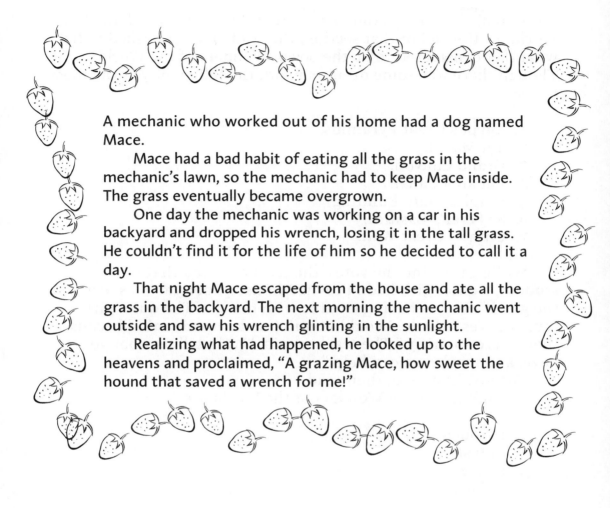

A mechanic who worked out of his home had a dog named Mace.

Mace had a bad habit of eating all the grass in the mechanic's lawn, so the mechanic had to keep Mace inside. The grass eventually became overgrown.

One day the mechanic was working on a car in his backyard and dropped his wrench, losing it in the tall grass. He couldn't find it for the life of him so he decided to call it a day.

That night Mace escaped from the house and ate all the grass in the backyard. The next morning the mechanic went outside and saw his wrench glinting in the sunlight.

Realizing what had happened, he looked up to the heavens and proclaimed, "A grazing Mace, how sweet the hound that saved a wrench for me!"

Gratitude

A group of geography students studied the Seven Wonders of the World. At the end of that section, the students were asked to list what *they* considered to be the Seven Wonders of the World. Though there was some disagreement, the following got the most votes:

1. Egypt's Great Pyramids,
2. Taj Mahal,
3. Grand Canyon,
4. Panama Canal,
5. Empire State Building,
6. St Peter's Basilica,
7. China's Great Wall.

While gathering the votes, the teacher noted that one student, a quiet girl, hadn't turned in her paper yet. So she asked the girl if she was having trouble with her list. The quiet girl replied, "Yes, a little. I couldn't quite make up my mind because there were so many." The teacher said, "Well, tell us what you have, and maybe we can help."

The girl hesitated, then read,
"I think the Seven Wonders of the World are...

1. to touch
2. to taste
3. to see
4. to hear

She hesitated a little, and then added,

5. to run
6. to laugh
7. and to love

It is far too easy for us to look at the exploits of man and refer to them as "wonders" while we overlook all God has done, regarding it as merely "ordinary". May you be reminded today of those things which are truly wondrous.

Greed

A young man once asked God how long a million years was to him. God replied, "A million years to me is just like a single second to you."

The young man asked God what a million dollars was to him. God replied, "A million dollars to me is just like a single penny to you."

Then the young man got his courage up and asked, "God, could I have one of your pennies?"

God smiled and replied, "Certainly, just a second."

Grief

When the Christian head teacher Philip Lawrence was killed just before Christmas 1996, his only son Lucien wrote the following message to Father Christmas:

Dear Father Christmas,

I hope you are well and not too cold. I hope you won't think that I am being a nuisance but I have changed my mind what I want for christmas. I wanted to have a telescope but now I want to have my daddy back because without my daddy to help I will not be able to see the stars anyway. I am the only boy in the family now but I am not very big and I need my daddy to help me to stop my mummy and sisters from crying.

love from

lucien lawrence

Age 8

Below is the text of the prayer that Lucien Lawrence recited at his father's funeral, complete with spelling mistakes:

God in Heaven,

Help us to think for a minit about the time when we all met my daddy.

Help us to think of his kindness. Not only was he a headmaster but he was my daddy too.

I remember the time he bort me something... Even thow it was too expensif.

The time he lernt me to spell words.

How gentle he was.

We played football in the hallway... even when he had lots of work to do.

Loving God, help us to pray that we will meet my daddy again.

Amen.

Growth

God loves you so much that He'll accept you just the way you are — but He loves you too much to leave you that way.

Hair

There's a new remedy for baldness on the market. It doesn't grow hair but it shrinks your head to fit what hair your head has left.

Grey hair is a sign of age not of wisdom. Greek proverb.

The best thing for grey hair is a sensible head.

There are three types of people. Those who are going bald at the front. Those who are going bald at the back. Those who are going bald in both places.

Those who are going bald at the front are sexy. Those who are going bald at the back are thinkers. And those who are going bald in both places THINK they are SEXY.

History

A survey has revealed a disconcerting ignorance of history among secondary school pupils, aged 11 to 18. Nearly two-thirds of those questioned did not know when the First World War started, and a small, but still worrying, four per cent thought that Adolf Hitler was British Prime Minister during the Second World War. A similar number thought that Oliver Cromwell had been a Battle of Britain air ace. More positively, half the children surveyed got all of the questions right, although the overall results are being greeted as evidence of the decline in core historical knowledge (18 January 2001). Some commentators argue that ignorance about history is a symptom of our postmodern culture, where facts are no longer considered to be absolutely knowable.

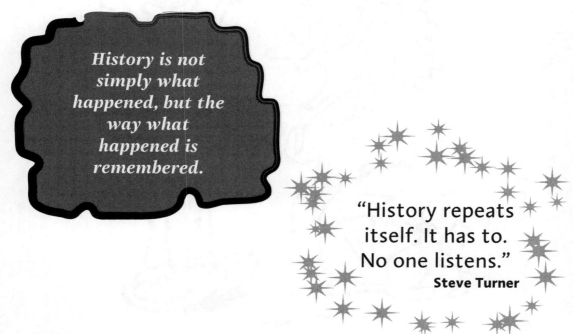

History is not simply what happened, but the way what happened is remembered.

"History repeats itself. It has to. No one listens."
Steve Turner

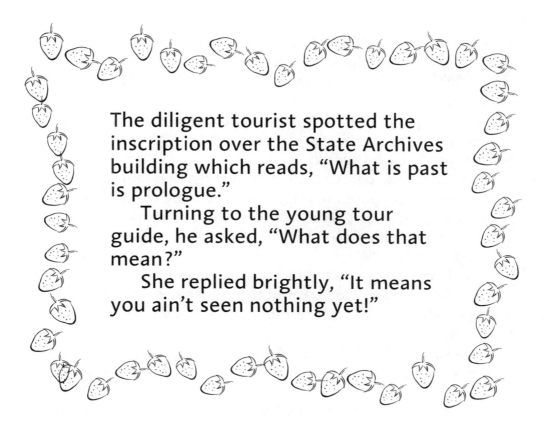

The diligent tourist spotted the inscription over the State Archives building which reads, "What is past is prologue."

Turning to the young tour guide, he asked, "What does that mean?"

She replied brightly, "It means you ain't seen nothing yet!"

Humanity

"A human being is part of the whole, called by us "Universe", a part limited in time and space.

"He experiences himself, his thoughts and feelings as something separated from the rest — a kind of optical delusion of consciousness.

"This delusion is a kind of prison for us, restricting us to our personal desires and to affection for a few persons nearest to us.

"Our task must be to free ourselves from this prison by widening our circle of compassion to embrace all living creatures and the whole nature in its beauty."

Albert Einstein

On the very first day, God created the cow. He said to the cow, "Today I have created you! As a cow, you must go to the field with the farmer all day long. You will work all day under the sun! I will give you a life span of 50 years."

Cow objected. "What? This kind of tough life you want me to live for 50 years? Let me have 20 years, and the 30 years I'll give back to you." So God agreed.

On the second day, God created the dog. God said to the dog, "What you are supposed to do is to sit all day by the door of your house. Any people that come in, you will have to bark at them! I'll give you a life span of 20 years."

Dog objected. "What? All day long to sit by the door? No way! I give you back ten years of life!" So God agreed.

On the third day, God created the monkey. He said to the monkey, "Monkey has to entertain people. You've got to make them laugh and do monkey tricks. I'll give you 20 years' life span."

Monkey objected. "What? Make them laugh? Do monkey faces and tricks? Ten years will do, and the other ten years I'll give you back." So God agreed.

On the fourth day, God created man and woman and said to them, "Your job is to sleep, eat, and play. There will be much to enjoy in your life. All you need to do is to enjoy things and do nothing. For this kind of life, I'll give you 20 years of life span."

The man objected. "What? Such a good life! Eat, play, sleep, do nothing? Enjoy the best and you expect me to live only for 20 years? No way. Why don't we make a deal? Since Cow gave you back 30 years, Dog gave you back ten years and Monkey gave you back ten years, I will take them from you! That makes my life span 70 years, right?" So God agreed.

AND THAT IS WHY… In our first 20 years, we eat, sleep, play, enjoy the best and do nothing much. For the next 30 years, we work all day long, suffer and get to support the family. For the next ten years, we entertain our grandchildren by making monkey faces and monkey tricks. And for the last ten years, we stay at home, sit in front of the door and bark at people.

Humility

At times it is important to remember just how small we are. Franklin D Roosevelt used to have a little ritual with the famous naturalist William Beebe. After an evening's chat the two men would go outside and look into the night sky. Gazing at the stars they would find the lower left-hand corner of the big square of Pegasus. One of them would recite these words as part of their ritual: "That is a spiral galaxy of Andromeda. It is as large as our Milky Way. It is one of a hundred million galaxies. It is 750,000 light years away. It consists of one hundred billion suns, each larger than our sun." They would then pause and Roosevelt would finally say, "Now I think we feel small enough. Let us go to bed."

Humility is to receive praise and to pass it on to God untouched.
J John

"God created the world out of nothing, and as long as we are nothing, he can make something out of us."
Martin Luther

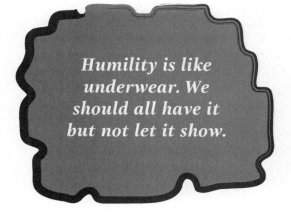

Humility is like underwear. We should all have it but not let it show.

The person who looks up to God rarely looks down on people.

"It is not a great thing to be humble when you are brought low, but to be humble when you are praised is a great and rare attainment."
St Bernard of Clairvaux

Humility is remaining teachable.

I

Ideas

"There is one thing stronger than all the armies in the world; an idea whose time has come."
Victor Hugo

Nothing dies more quickly than a new idea in a closed mind.

"Only ideas that we actually live by are of any value."
Herman Hesse

"A person's mind stretched by a new idea never goes back to its original dimensions."
Oliver Wendell Holmes

Don't just entertain new ideas. Put them to work!

Initiative

A rumpled man walks into a bank in New York City and asks for the loan officer. He says he is going to Europe on business for two weeks and needs to borrow $5,000. The bank officer says the bank will need some kind of security for such a loan. So the man — clearly an eccentric — hands over the keys to a new Rolls Royce parked on the street in front of the bank. Everything checks out, and the bank agrees to accept the car as collateral for the loan. An employee drives the Rolls into the bank's underground garage and parks it there.

Two weeks later, the man returns, repays the $5,000 and the interest, which comes to $15.41. The loan officer says, "We are very happy to have had your business, and this transaction has worked out very nicely, but we are a little puzzled. While you were away, we checked you out and found that you are a multi-millionaire. What puzzles us is why would you bother to borrow $5,000?"

The man replies, "Where else in New York can I park my car for two weeks for $15?"

If there is no wind, then row!

"No one knows what he can do till he tries."

Publius Syrus

The journey of a thousand miles begins with a single step.

Chinese proverb

Two men are being chased by a bear when one stops to put on his trainers.

The other man yells, "You idiot! You can't outrun a bear!"

The first man gasps, "I don't have to outrun a bear. I just have to outrun you!"

Inspiration

Internet

You know you're addicted to the internet when...

1. You wake up at 3am to go to the bathroom and stop to check your e-mail on the way back to bed.
2. You get a tattoo that reads "This body best viewed with Microsoft Internet Explorer 3.0 or higher".
3. You name your children Eudora, Mozilla and Dotcom.
4. You turn off your modem and get this awful empty feeling, like you just pulled the plug on a loved one.
5. You spend half of the plane trip with your laptop on your lap and your child in the overhead compartment.
6. You decide to stay in college for an additional year or two, just for the free internet access.
7. You laugh at people with 9600-baud modems.
8. You start using smilies in your snail mail.
9. Your hard drive crashes. You haven't logged in for two hours. You...
   — start to twitch.
   — pick up the phone and manually dial your ISP's access number.
   — try to hum to communicate with the modem...and succeed.
10. You find yourself typing "com" after every full stop when using a word processor.com
11. You refer to going to the bathroom as downloading.
12. You start introducing yourself as "JohnDoe at AOL dot com".
13. All of your friends have an @ in their name.
14. Your cat has its own home page.
15. You can't call your mother. She doesn't have a modem.
16. You check your mail. It says "no new messages" so you check it again.
17. Your phone bill comes to your doorstep in a box.
18. You don't know what sexes three of your closest friends are, because they have neutral nicknames and you never bothered to ask.
19. You move into a new house and decide to Netscape before you landscape.
20. You start tilting your head sideways to smile.

J

Jesus

Maybe Jesus was more Jewish than Greek
He went into his father's business
He lived at home until he was 33
He was sure His mother was a virgin and His Mother was sure He was God

Maybe Jesus was Irish
He never got married
He was always telling stories
He loved green pastures

Maybe Jesus was Puerto Rican
His first name was Jesus
He was bilingual
He was always being harassed by the authorities

Maybe Jesus was Italian
He talked with his hands
He had wine with every meal
He worked in the building trade

Maybe Jesus was black
He called everybody brother
He liked Gospel
He couldn't get a fair trial

Maybe Jesus was a Californian
He never cut his hair
He walked around barefoot
He started a new religion

An old legend:
A man fell into quicksand and started to sink. While he was sinking, Confucius walked by and said, "There is evidence that men should stay out of such places". But the man was still sinking in quicksand. Then Buddha walked by and said, "Let that man be a lesson to the world". But the man was still sinking in quicksand. Then Mohammed walked by and said, "Alas, it is the will of Allah". But the man was still sinking in quicksand. Then a Hindu walked by and said, "Never mind, you will return to earth in another form". But the man was still sinking in quicksand.

Finally Jesus walked by and reached out His hand and said, "Grab hold of my hand and I will pull you out."

> *"The whole of history is incomprehensible without Jesus."*
>
> **Ernest Renan**

He was born in an obscure village, the child of a peasant woman. He grew up in yet another village, where he worked in a carpenter's shop till he was thirty. Then for three years he was an itinerant preacher.

He never wrote a book. He never held an office. He never had a family or owned a house. He didn't go to college. He never travelled more than 200 miles from the place where he was born. He did none of the things one usually associates with greatness. He had no credentials but himself.

He was only thirty-three when the tide of public opinion turned against him. His friends ran away. He was nailed to a cross between two thieves. While he was dying, his executioners gambled for his clothing, the only property he had on earth.

Twenty centuries have come and gone and today he is the central figure of the human race. All the armies that ever marched, all the navies that ever sailed, all the parliaments that ever sat, all the kings that ever reigned, put together, have not affected the life of man on this earth as much as that one solitary life.

Anon, printed as a newspaper advert

THEY MISSED HIM! They were looking for a lion, He came as a Lamb, and they missed Him.

They were looking for a warrior, He came as a Peacemaker, and they missed Him.

They were looking for a king, He came as a Servant, and they missed Him.

They were looking for liberation from Rome, He submitted to the Roman stake, and they missed Him.

They were looking for a fit to their mould, He was the mould breaker, and they missed Him.

Will you?

Joy

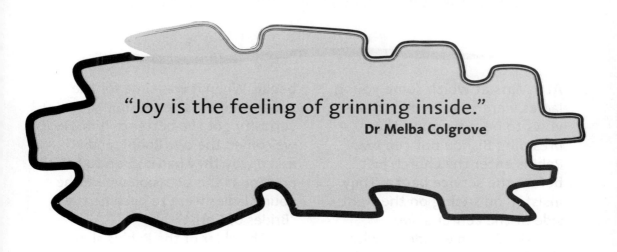

"Joy is the feeling of grinning inside."
Dr Melba Colgrove

Judaism

The Chief Rabbi of Israel and the Pope are in a meeting in Rome. The Rabbi notices an unusually fancy phone on a side table in the Pope's private chambers. "What is that phone for?" he asks the pontiff. "It's my direct line to the Lord!" the Pope replies. The Rabbi is skeptical, and the Pope notices. The Holy Father insists that the Rabbi try it out, and, indeed, he is connected to the Lord. The Rabbi holds a lengthy discussion with Him. After hanging up the Rabbi says, "Thank you very much. This is great! But listen, I want to pay for my phone charges." The Pope of course refuses, but the Rabbi is steadfast and finally the pontiff gives in. He checks the counter on the phone and says: "All right! The charges were 100,000 Lira (£40)." The Chief Rabbi gladly hands over a packet of bills.

A few months later, the Pope is in Jerusalem on an official visit. In the Chief Rabbi's chambers he sees a phone identical to his and learns it also is a direct line to the Lord. The Pope remembers he has an urgent matter that requires divine consultation and asks if he can use the Rabbi's phone. The Rabbi gladly agrees, hands him the phone, and the Pope chats away. After hanging up, the Pope offers to pay the phone charges. This time, the Chief Rabbi refuses to accept payment. After the Pope insists, the Chief Rabbi relents and looks on the phone counter and says: "1 Shekel 50! (20p)." The Pope looks surprised: "Why so cheap!?" The Rabbi smiles and says, "It's a local call from here."

At a Mass at which some young ladies were to take their final vows to become nuns, the presiding Bishop noticed two Rabbis enter the church just before the service began. They insisted on sitting on the right side of the center aisle.

The Bishop wondered why they had come, but he didn't have time to inquire before the Mass began. When it was time for the announcements, the Bishop's curiosity got the better of him. He welcomed the two Rabbis and asked why they had chosen to be present at this occasion where the young ladies were to become the "Brides of Christ".

The elder of the Rabbis slowly rose to his feet and explained, "Family of the Groom".

At the Henry Street Hebrew School, Goldblatt, the new teacher, finished the day's lesson. It was now time for the usual question period. "Mr Goldblatt," announced little Joey, "there's somethin' I can't figure out."

"What's that Joey?" asked Goldblatt.

"Well accordin' to the Bible, the Children of Israel crossed the Red Sea, right?"

"Right."

"An' the Children of Israel beat up the Philistines, right?"

"Er—right."

"An' the Children of Israel built the Temple, right?"

"Again you're right."

"An' the Children of Israel fought the 'gyptians, an' the Children of Israel fought the Romans, an' the Children of Israel wuz always doin' somethin' important, right?"

"All that is right, too," agreed Goldblatt. "So what's your question?"

"What I wanna know is this," demanded Joey. "What wuz all the grown-ups doin' all that time?"

Justice

"Justice is truth in action."
Joseph Joubert

If a cause is just, it will eventually triumph in spite of all the propaganda issued against it.

"I tremble for my country when I reflect that God is just."
Thomas Jefferson

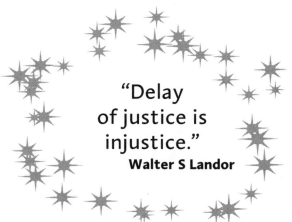

"Delay of justice is injustice."
Walter S Landor

Once the game is over, the king and the pawn go back in the same box.

Justice is like fire; if one covers it with a veil, it still burns.

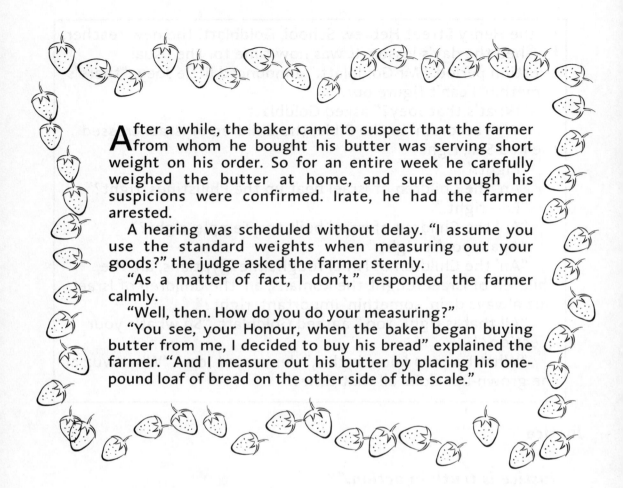

After a while, the baker came to suspect that the farmer from whom he bought his butter was serving short weight on his order. So for an entire week he carefully weighed the butter at home, and sure enough his suspicions were confirmed. Irate, he had the farmer arrested.

A hearing was scheduled without delay. "I assume you use the standard weights when measuring out your goods?" the judge asked the farmer sternly.

"As a matter of fact, I don't," responded the farmer calmly.

"Well, then. How do you do your measuring?"

"You see, your Honour, when the baker began buying butter from me, I decided to buy his bread" explained the farmer. "And I measure out his butter by placing his one-pound loaf of bread on the other side of the scale."

K

Kindness

One day, a poor boy who was selling goods from door to door to pay his way through school found he had only one penny left, and he was hungry. He decided he would ask for a meal at the next house. However, he lost his nerve when a lovely young woman opened the door. Instead of a meal he asked for a drink of water. She thought he looked hungry so she brought him a large glass of milk. He drank it slowly, and then asked, "How much do I owe you?"

"You don't owe me anything," she replied. "Mother has taught us never to accept pay for a kindness."

He said, "Then I thank you from my heart."

As Howard Kelly left that house, he not only felt stronger physically, but his faith in God and people was stronger also. He had been ready to give up and quit.

Years later that same woman became critically ill. The local doctors were baffled. They finally sent her to the big city, where they called in specialists to study her rare disease. Dr Howard Kelly was called in for the consultation. When he heard the name of the town she came from, a strange light filled his eyes. Immediately he rose and went down the hall of the hospital to her room. Dressed in his doctor's gown he went in to see her. He recognized her at once. He went back to the consultation room determined to do his best to save her life. From that day he gave special attention to the case. After a long struggle, the battle was won.

Dr Kelly asked the hospital to pass the patient's bill to him for approval. He looked at it, then wrote something on the edge and the bill was sent to her room. She feared to open it, for she was sure it would take the rest of her life to pay for it all. Finally she looked, and something caught her attention on the side of the bill. She read these words: "Paid in full with one glass of milk."

(Signed) Dr Howard Kelly

"I expect to pass through life but once. If, therefore, there be any kindness I can show, or any good thing I can do to any fellow being, let me do it now, for I shall not pass this way again."

William Penn

"Kindness is a language the dumb can speak and the deaf can hear and understand."

Christian Nestel Bovee

Kindness is the oil that takes the friction out of life.

Don't expect to enjoy the cream of life if you keep your milk of human kindness all bottled up.

Kindness pays most when you don't do it for pay.

Be kind to everybody. You never know who might show up in the jury at your trial.

The person who sows seeds of kindness will have a perpetual harvest.

"Wherever there are people, there is an opportunity for kindness."
J.John

Never part without kind words. They might be your last.

"So how are things down on earth?" asked St Peter of the beggar who had just arrived at the Pearly Gates. "Did people treat you decently?"

"Oh, they were kind enough", responded the beggar mournfully. "But even the kind ones never seemed to have any money."

The self-absorbed parishioner was told by her priest to go to her community and do something kind for a needy person.

Unable to bring herself to actually approach one of the local unfortunates, she scribbled, "Best of luck", on a £20 note and thrust it into the nearest hand.

The next day she was startled when the same man approached his benefactor.

"Nice work, lady", he said cheerfully. "Best of Luck paid ten to one."

Knowledge

During the years of the Great Depression in America, a man called Yates owned a huge amount of land in Texas. He raised sheep on it. He lived in great poverty and barely had enough money for food and clothing for himself and his family. Soon it looked as if he would have to sell up.

One day an oil company worker approached him. "We think there may be oil on your land," he said. "Will you let us drill on it?"

Yates thought he had nothing to lose so he said yes. At a very shallow depth, the drill struck the largest deposit of oil that had ever been discovered in the whole of North America. 80,000 barrels of oil were produced per day! Overnight, Yates became a billionaire! Actually, Yates had been a billionaire ever since he had owned the land. He just didn't know it!

The person who knows everything has the most to learn.

Strange how much you've got to know, before you know how little you know.

Education is forcing abstract ideas into concrete heads.

"To be conscious that you are ignorant is a great step to knowledge."
Benjamin Disraeli

Knowing without doing is like sowing without plowing.

"As for me, all I know is that I know nothing."
Socrates

Last Words

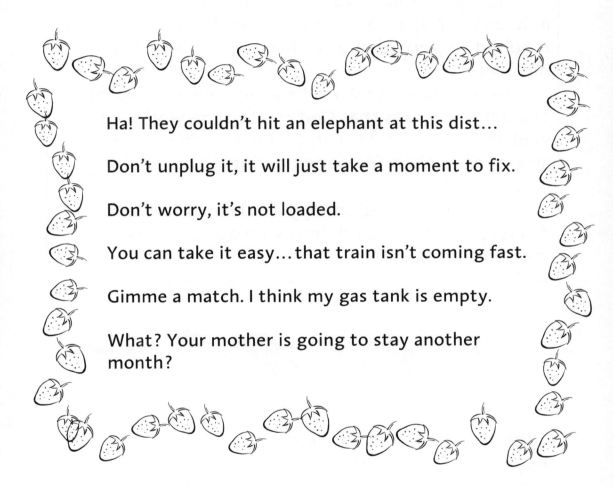

Ha! They couldn't hit an elephant at this dist...

Don't unplug it, it will just take a moment to fix.

Don't worry, it's not loaded.

You can take it easy...that train isn't coming fast.

Gimme a match. I think my gas tank is empty.

What? Your mother is going to stay another month?

Lawyers

Three professional men were arguing which of them belonged to the oldest profession.

The doctor said, "Well, the Bible says that God took a rib out of Adam to make a woman. Since that clearly required surgery, then the oldest profession is surely medicine."

The engineer shook his head and replied, "No, no. The Bible also says that God created the world out of void and chaos. To do that, God must surely have been an engineer. Therefore, engineering is the oldest profession."

The lawyer smiled smugly and leaned forward discreetly. "Ah," he said, "but who do you think created the chaos?"

Judge to prisoner in the dock — "Would you like a lawyer to defend you?"

Prisoner: "There's no need. The Lord is my defender."

Judge: "I think you'd do better to have someone better known locally."

As reported in a legal journal, the following are 22 questions actually asked of witnesses by barristers during trials together with, in certain cases, the responses given by insightful witnesses:

1. "Now doctor, isn't it true that when a person dies in their sleep, they don't know about it until the next morning?"

2. "The youngest son, the 20-year-old, how old is he?"

3. "Were you present when your picture was taken?"

4. "Were you alone or by yourself?"

5. "Was it you or your younger brother who was killed in the war?"

6. "Did he kill you?"

7. "How far apart were the vehicles at the time of the collision?"

8. "You were there until the time you left, is that true?"

9. "How many times have you committed suicide?"

10. Q: "So the date of conception (of the baby) was August 8th?"
    A: "Yes."
    Q: "And what were you doing at that time?"

11. Q: "She had three children, right?"
    A: "Yes."
    Q: "How many were boys?"
    A: "None."
    Q: "Were there any girls?"

12. Q: "You say the stairs went down to the basement?"
    A: "Yes."

Q: "And these stairs, did they go up also?"

13. Q: "Mr Slattery, you went on a rather elaborate honeymoon, didn't you?"
    A: "I went to Europe, Sir."
    Q: "And you took your new wife?"

14. Q: "How was your first marriage terminated?"
    A: "By death."
    Q: "And whose death was it that terminated the marriage?"

15. Q: "Can you describe the individual?"
    A: "He was about medium height and had a beard."
    Q: "Was this a male, or a female?"

16. Q: "Is your appearance here this morning pursuant to a notice which I sent to your barrister?"
    A: "No, this is how I dress when I go to work."

17. Q: "Doctor, how many autopsies have you performed on dead people?"
    A: "All my autopsies are performed on dead people."

18. Q: "All your responses must be oral, OK? What school did you go to?"
    A: "Oral."

19. Q: "Do you recall the time that you examined the body?"

    A: "The autopsy started around 8:30pm."

    Q: "And Mr Dennington was dead at the time?"

    A: "No, he was sitting on the table wondering why I was doing an autopsy."

20. Q: "You were not shot in the fracas?"

    A: "No, I was shot midway between the fracas and the navel."

21. Q: "Are you qualified to give a urine sample?"

    A: "I have been since early childhood."

22. Q: "Doctor, before you performed the autopsy, did you check for a pulse?"

    A: "No."

    Q: "Did you check for blood pressure?"

    A: "No."

    Q: "Did you check for breathing?"

    A: "No."

    Q: "So, then it is possible that the patient was alive when you began the autopsy?"

    A: "No."

    Q: "How can you be so sure, Doctor?"

    A: "Because his brain was sitting on my desk in a jar."

    Q: "But could the patient have still been alive nevertheless?"

    A: "It is possible that he could have been alive and practicing law somewhere."

Leadership

"What makes a leader — intelligence, integrity, imagination, skill or statecraft? None of these. It's the fact that a person has a following.
G W Johnson

"It's skill not strength that governs a ship."
Thomas Fuller

"No one is fit to command another that cannot command themselves."
William Penn

Part of the college application was directed to the applicant's parents, and one of the questions was, "Would you consider your child to be a leader or a follower?"

After much deliberation, the father wrote that he felt his son, although very much a unique individual, was really more of a follower.

Not long after, a letter of acceptance arrived from the college, accompanied by a note from the Registrar, welcoming his child.

"We feel he'll fit in especially well," the letter read, "as he will be the only follower in a class of 249 leaders!"

Lent

An Irishman walks into a Dublin bar, orders three pints of Guinness and sits in a corner of the room, taking a sip out of each glass in turn. When all three pint glasses are empty, he returns to the bar and orders three more. The bartender advises him: "You know, a pint goes flat after it's drawn. It would taste better if you bought one at a time.

The Irishman replies: "Well, you see, I have two brothers — one in America, the other in Australia and I'm here in Dublin. When we all left home, we promised to always drink this way to remember the days when we drank together."

The bartender admits that this is a touching custom and leaves it at that. Over the next few weeks the Irishman becomes a regular at the bar, always drinking the same way: ordering three pints of Guinness at a time and drinking them in turn.

One day, he comes in and orders only two pints. The other regulars notice and fall silent. When he returns to the bar for the second round, the bartender says: "I don't want to intrude on your grief, but I wanted to offer my condolences and those of our regulars on your sad loss."

The Irishman looks confused for a moment before the light dawns and he laughs. "Oh, no," he says, "everyone's fine but I've stopped drinking for Lent."

Life

"If you want my final opinion on the mystery of life and all that, I can give it to you in a nutshell. The universe is like a safe to which there is a combination, but the combination is in the safe."

Peter De Vries

"There are two ways to live your life. One is though nothing is a miracle. The other is as though everything is a miracle."
Albert Einstein

Lucy was talking to Charlie Brown one day.

"Charlie Brown," she asked, "You see that hill?"

"Yes, I see it," said Charlie Brown.

Lucy said, "Charlie Brown, on the other side of the hill is happiness. Some day I am going to climb that hill and I am going to get to the other side and I expect to find all the answers to life on the other side. I expect to find meaning and purpose, joy and happiness on the other side of that hill."

Charlie Brown scratched his head. "Do you suppose," he mused, "that there is a kid on the other side of that hill looking over to our side and saying to someone else, 'All the answers to life are on the other side of that hill?' What if some day he climbs across that hill and comes across to our side looking for happiness and meaning and purpose and all the answers to life?"

Lucy looked at Charlie Brown and then she looked at that hill and said, "Forget it, kid, the answer is not over here."

Lightbulb Jokes

How many AMISH does it take to change a light bulb?
What's a light bulb?

How many BAPTISTS does it take to change a light bulb?
Change? Who said anything about change?

How many CALVINISTS does it take to change a light bulb?
None: God has predestined when the light will be on. Calvinists do not change light bulbs. They simply read the instructions and pray that their light bulb will be the one that has been chosen to be changed.

How many CATHOLICS does it take to change a light bulb?
None. They use candles.

How many CHARISMATICS does it take to change a light bulb?

Ten: one to change the bulb and nine to pray against the spirit of darkness.

How many INDEPENDENT FUNDAMENTALISTS does it take to change a light bulb?

Only one, because any more might result in too much co-operation.

How many LIBERALS does it take to change a light bulb?

At least ten, as they need to hold a debate on whether or not the light bulb exists. Even if they can agree upon the existence of the light bulb, they still might not change it, to keep from alienating those who might use other forms of light.

How many MEMBERS OF AN ESTABLISHED BIBLE-TEACHING CHURCH THAT IS OVER 20 YEARS OLD does it take to change a light bulb?

One to actually change the bulb, and nine to say how much they liked the old one.

How many METHODISTS does it take to change a light bulb?

This statement was issued: "We choose not to make a statement either in favour of or against the need for a light bulb. However, if in your own journey you have found that a light bulb works for you, that's fine. You are invited to write a poem or compose a modern dance about your personal relationship with your light bulb (or light source, or non-dark resource), and present it next month at our annual light-bulb Sunday service, in which we explore a number of light-bulb traditions, including incandescent, fluorescent, three-way, long-life, and tinted — all of which are equally valid paths to luminescence."

How many SOUTHERN BAPTISTS does it take to change a light bulb?

At least 109: Seven on the Light Bulb Task Force Sub-committee who report to the twelve on the Light Bulb Task Force, appointed by the 15 on the Trustee Board. Their recommendation is reviewed by the Finance Committee Executive of five, who place it on the agenda of the 18-member Finance committee. If they approve, they bring a motion to the 27-member Church Board, who appoint another twelve-member review committee. If they recommend that the Church Board proceed, a resolution is brought to the

Congregational Business Meeting. They appoint another eight-member review committee. If their report to the next Congregational Business Meeting supports the changing of the light bulb, and the congregation votes in favour, the responsibility to carry out the light bulb change is passed on to the Trustee Board, who in turn appoint a seven-member committee to find the best price on new light bulbs. Their recommendation of which hardware store has the best buy must then be reviewed by the 23-member Ethics Committee to make certain that this hardware store has no connections to Disneyland. They report back to the Trustee Board who then commissions the Trustee in charge of the janitor to ask him to make the change. By then the janitor discovers that one more light bulb has burned out.

How many TELEVANGELISTS does it take to change a light bulb?
One. But for the message of light to continue, send in your donation today.

How many YOUTH PASTORS does it take to change a light bulb?
Youth pastors aren't around long enough for a light bulb to burn out.

Longevity

An old man was relaxing at his hundredth birthday party when a reporter went up to him. "Sir, what is the secret of your long life?"

The man considered this for a moment, then replied, "Every day at 9pm I have a glass of port. Good for the heart."

The reporter replied, "That's ALL?"

The man smiled, "That, and cancelling my voyage on the *Titanic*."

Love

A story is told about a soldier who was finally coming home after having fought in Vietnam. He called his parents from San Francisco.

"Mom and Dad, I'm coming home, but I've a favor to ask. I have a friend I'd like to bring home with me."

"Sure," they replied, "we'd love to meet him."

"There's something you should know," the son continued. "He was hurt pretty badly in the fighting. He stepped on a land mine and lost an arm and a leg. He has nowhere else to go, and I want him to come live with us."

"I'm sorry to hear that, son. Maybe we can help him find somewhere to live."

"No, Mom and Dad, I want him to live with us."

"Son," said the father, "you don't know what you're asking. Someone with such a handicap would be a terrible burden on us. We have our own lives to live, and we can't let something like this interfere with our lives. I think you should just come home and forget about this guy. He'll find a way to live on his own."

At that point, the son hung up the phone. The parents heard nothing more from him. A few days later, however, they received a call from the San Francisco police. Their son had died after falling from a building, they were told. The police believed it was suicide. The grief-stricken parents flew to San Francisco and were taken to the city morgue to identify the body of their son. They recognized him, but to their horror they also discovered something they didn't know: their son had only one arm and one leg.

My grandparents were married for over half a century, and played their own special game from the time they first met. The goal of their game was to write the word "shmily" in a surprise place for the other to find. They took turns leaving "shmily" around the house, and as soon as one of them discovered it, it was their turn to hide it once more.

They dragged "shmily" with their fingers through the sugar and flour containers to await whoever was preparing the next meal. They smeared it in the dew on the windows overlooking the patio where my grandma always fed us warm milk. "Shmily" was written in the steam left on the mirror after a hot shower, where it would reappear bath after bath. At one point, my grandmother even unrolled an entire roll of toilet paper to leave "shmily" on the very last sheet.

There was no end to the places "shmily" would pop up. Little notes with "shmily" scribbled hurriedly were found on dashboards and car seats, or taped to steering wheels. The notes were stuffed inside shoes and left under pillows. "Shmily" was written in the dust upon the mantel and traced in the ashes of the fireplace. This mysterious word was as much a part of my grandparents' house as the furniture.

But there was a dark cloud in my grandparents' life: my grandmother had breast cancer. The disease had first appeared ten years earlier. As always, Grandpa was with her every step of the way. He comforted her in their yellow room, painted that way so that she could always be surrounded by sunshine, even when she was too sick to go outside.

Now the cancer was again attacking her body. With the help of a cane and my grandfather's steady hand, they went to church every morning. But my grandmother grew steadily weaker until, finally, she could not leave the house anymore. For a while, Grandpa would go to church alone, praying to God to watch over his wife. Then one day, what we all dreaded finally happened. Grandma was gone.

"Shmily." It was scrawled in yellow on the pink ribbons of my grandmother's funeral bouquet. As the crowd thinned and the last mourners turned to leave, my aunts, uncles, cousins and other family members came forward and gathered around Grandma one last time. Grandpa stepped up to my grandmother's casket and, taking a shaky breath, he began to sing to her. Through his tears and grief, the song came, a deep and throaty lullaby.

Shaking with my own sorrow, I will never forget that moment. For I knew that, although I couldn't begin to fathom the depth of their love, I had been privileged to witness its unmatched beauty.

S-h-m-i-l-y: See How Much I Love You.

"Love cures people: the ones who receive love, and the ones who give it too."
Dr Karl A Menninger

The supreme happiness of life is the conviction that we are loved.

Lying

> The preacher told his congregation, "Next Sunday my sermon will be on the sin of lying. To prepare yourselves please read the seventeenth chapter of Mark."
>
> The following Sunday arrived and he asked, "How many of you read the seventeenth chapter of Mark?"
>
> Most of the congregation raised their hands.
>
> "Good," he replied. "There are only 16 chapters in Mark. Now for the sermon on the sin of lying."

Marriage

The price of love is going up. According to a new survey, the average wedding in the UK this year cost a record £11,268.

Newlyweds in London dig deepest for their big day, spending an average £14,323, while couples in the South West are most budget-conscious, spending £9,167.

A couple in the capital can on average spend £4,222 on catering, £1,698 on rings, £920 on video and photography, £808 on the wedding dress and £299 on flowers.

As the average cost of weddings goes up so does the age of brides and grooms — on average women now tie the knot aged 28 and men at 31.

Most couples now live together longer before marrying but enjoy relatively short engagements lasting just 12 months.

The annual Cost of Love survey by *Wedding and Home* magazine also revealed that tradition is making a comeback with 60% of couples opting for a big church wedding, up 5% on the previous year.

It also found 91% of men choose to wear a ring to mark their commitment to their new wife.

Wedding and Home editor Christine Hayes said: "The survey also shows that, in the majority of cases, couples make a significant contribution towards the wedding costs rather than leaving it all to the bride's dad.

"This means they have greater control over the day and can adapt tradition to suit themselves. They want their big day to reflect their own style and personalities and are prepared to pay to do so."

A married couple trying to live up to a snobbish lifestyle went to a party. The conversation turned to Mozart. "Absolutely brilliant, magnificent, a genius!"

The woman, wanting to join in the conversation, remarked casually, "Ah, Mozart. You're so right. I love him. Only this morning I saw him getting on the No. 5 bus to Chelsea."

There was a sudden hush, and everyone looked at her. Her husband was mortified. He pulled her away and whispered, "We're leaving right now. Get your coat and let's get out of here."

As they drove home, he kept muttering to himself. Finally his wife turned to him. "You're angry about something."

"Oh really? You noticed?" he sneered. "I've never been so embarrassed in my life! You saw Mozart take the No. 5 bus to Chelsea? You idiot! Don't you know the No. 5 bus doesn't go to Chelsea?"

Adam and Eve had an ideal marriage. He didn't have to hear about all the men she could have married, and she didn't hear about how well his mother cooked!

Ten Commandments for Marriage:

1. Thou shalt not take thy partner for granted
2. Thou shalt not expect perfection of each other
3. Thou shalt be patient, loving, understanding, kind and true
4. Thou shalt tend the garden of love daily
5. Thou shalt take great care that thy partner's trust shall never be violated or diminished in any way
6. Thou shalt not forget thy wedding vows, remembering especially those important words, "FOR BETTER OR WORSE"
7. Thou shalt not hide thy true feelings. Mutual love provides a bright sunlit room where things of the heart can be discussed freely and without fear
8. Thou shalt always respect each other as individuals. Degrading words and a sharp tongue cause grave distortions. Endearing terms ennoble, lift up and engender peace
9. Thou shalt give thy marriage room to grow. Both partners should be willing to face the future together with confidence and trust; today is a better day for them than yesterday, and tomorrow will find them closer still
10. Thou shalt through all thy days reverence God thy creator, never forgetting that it is he who made you one.

One of the most remarkable examples of lifelong marital commitment we have come across is from a recent Ann Landers column in the States:

Dear Ann Landers:

I'm going to tell you about a love story that I witness every time I go to the nursing home to see my husband, who has Alzheimer's disease. Unfortunately, I know firsthand how this terrible illness affects family members, but I would like the world to know what love really is.

I see a man who, I understand, has spent the last eight years caring for his wife, who has Alzheimer's. They have been married over 50 years. He cooks and feeds her every bite of food she eats. He has bathed her and dressed her every day all these years. They have no other family. She lost a baby at birth, and they never had any more children.

I cannot describe the tenderness and love that man shows for his wife. She is unable to recognize anyone, including him. The only things she shows any interest in are two baby dolls. They are never out of her hands.

I observed him when I parked my car beside his the other day. He sat in his old pickup truck for a few minutes, then he patted down what little hair he had, straightened the threadbare collar of his shirt and looked in the mirror for a final check before going in to see his wife. It was as if he were courting her. They have been partners all these years and have seen each other under all kinds of circumstances, yet he carefully groomed himself before he called on his wife, who wouldn't even know him.

Meaning of Life

The following statement is purposefully without punctuation; we suggest you put it on an OHP in the following format, then read it out in the two entirely different ways suggested below:

He is a young man yet experienced in vice and wickedness he is never found in opposing the works of iniquity he takes delight in the downfall of his neighbors he never rejoices in the prosperity of his fellow creatures he is always ready to assist in destroying the peace of society he takes no pleasure in serving the Lord he is uncommonly diligent in sowing discord among his friends and acquaintances he takes no pride in laboring to promote the cause of Christianity he has not been negligent in endeavoring to tear down the church he makes no effort to subdue his evil passions he strives hard to build up Satan's kingdom he lends no aid to the support of the gospel among the heathen he contributes largely to the devil he will never go to heaven he must go where he will receive his just reward

He is a young man/ yet experienced in vice and wickedness/ he is never found in opposing the works of iniquity/ he takes delight in the downfall of his neighbors/ he never rejoices in the prosperity of his fellow creatures/ he is always ready to assist in destroying the peace of society/ he takes no pleasure in serving the Lord/ he is uncommonly diligent in sowing discord among his friends and acquaintances/ he takes no pride in laboring to promote the cause of Christianity/ he has not been negligent in endeavoring to tear down the church/ he makes no effort to subdue his evil passions/ he strives hard to build up Satan's kingdom/ he lends no aid to the support of the gospel among the heathen/ he contributes largely to the devil/ he will never go to heaven/ he must go where he will receive his just reward

Now try reading the same statement this way:

He is a young man yet experienced/ in vice and wickedness he is never found/ in opposing the works of iniquity he takes delight/ in the downfall of his neighbors he never rejoices/ in the prosperity of his fellow creatures he is always ready to assist/ in destroying the peace of society he takes no pleasure/ in serving the Lord he is uncommonly diligent/ in sowing discord among his friends and acquaintances he takes no pride/ in laboring to promote the cause of Christianity he has not been negligent/ in endeavoring to tear down the church he makes no effort/ to subdue his evil passions he strives hard/ to build up Satan's kingdom he lends no aid/ to the support of the gospel among the heathen he contributes largely/ to the devil he will never go/ to heaven he must go/ where he will receive his just reward

Medicine

Things You Don't Want To Hear In Surgery

1. Someone call the janitor — we're going to need a mop.
2. Bo! Bo! Come back with that! Bad Dog!
3. Wait a minute, if this is his spleen, then what's that?
4. Hand me that... er... that er... thingy.
5. Oh no! I just lost my Rolex.
6. Hey, has anyone ever survived 500ml of this stuff before?
7. Drat, there go the lights again.
8. Y'know, there's big money in kidneys. Hey, this bloke's got two of 'em.
9. Everybody stand back! I lost my contact lens!
10. What's this doing here?
11. I wish I hadn't forgotten my glasses.
12. Sterile, shmeril. The floor's clean, right?
13. OK, now take a picture from this angle.
14. What do you mean "You want a divorce"!
15. Blow it! Page 47 of the manual is missing!

In the beginning there was Adam…

So God asked him, "What is wrong with you?"

Adam said he didn't have anyone to talk to. God said that He was going to make Adam a companion and that it would be a woman.

God said, "This person will gather food for you, cook for you, and when you discover clothing she'll wash it for you. She will always agree with every decision you make. She will bear your children and never ask you to get up in the middle of the night to take care of them. She will not nag you and will always be the first to admit she was wrong when you've had a disagreement. She will never have a headache and will freely give you love and passion whenever you need it."

Adam asked God, "What will a woman like that cost?"

God replied, "An arm and a leg."

Then Adam asked, "What can I get for a rib?"

The rest is history.

The Real Man Test (Note: All "real men" answer "C" to all of these questions)

1. Aliens from a highly advanced society visit the Earth, and you are the first human they encounter. As a token of intergalactic friendship, they present you with a small but incredibly sophisticated device that is capable of curing all disease, providing an infinite supply of clean energy, wiping out hunger and poverty, and permanently eliminating oppression and violence all over the entire Earth.

    You decide to:

    A. Present it to the President of the United States.
    B. Present it to the Secretary General of the United Nations.
    C. Take it apart.

2. In your opinion, the ideal pet is:

    A. A cat.
    B. A dog.
    C. A dog that eats cats.

3. One weekday morning your wife wakes up feeling ill and asks you to get your three children ready for school. Your first question to her is:

    A. "Do they need to eat or anything?"
    B. "They're in school already?"
    C. "There are three of them?"

4. What, in your opinion, is the most reasonable explanation for the fact that Moses led the Israelites all over the place for 40 years before they finally got to the Promised Land?

    A. He was being tested.
    B. He wanted them to really appreciate the Promised Land when they finally got there.
    C. He refused to ask for directions.

Men and Women

A man will pay £2 for a £1 item he needs. A woman will pay £1 for a £2 item that she doesn't need.

A woman worries about the future until she gets a husband. A man never worries about the future until he gets a wife.

Ministers

One of the toughest tasks a church faces is choosing a minister.

A member of an official board undergoing this painful process finally lost patience. He'd just witnessed the Pastoral Relations Committee reject applicant after applicant for some minor fault — real or imagined. It was time for a bit of soul-searching on the part of the committee. So he stood up and read this letter purporting to be from another applicant.

Gentlemen: Understanding your pulpit is vacant, I should like to apply for the position. I have many qualifications. I've been a preacher with much success and also had some success as a writer. Some say I'm a good organizer. I've been a leader most places I've been.

I'm over 50 years of age and have never preached in one place for more than three years. In some places, I have left town after my work caused riots and disturbances. I must admit I have been in jail three or four times, but not because of any real wrongdoing.

My health is not too good, though I still accomplish a great deal. The churches I have preached in have been small, though located in several large cities.

I've not gotten along well with religious leaders in the towns where I have preached. In fact, some have threatened me, and even attacked me physically. I am not too good at keeping records. I have been known to forget who I have baptized.

However, if you can use me, I promise to do my best for you.

The board member turned to the committee and said, "Well, what do you think? Shall we call him?"

The good church folks were appalled! Consider a sickly, troublemaking, absent-minded ex-jailbird? Was the board member crazy? Who signed the application? Who had such colossal nerve?

The board member eyed them all keenly before he replied, "It's signed, 'The Apostle Paul'."

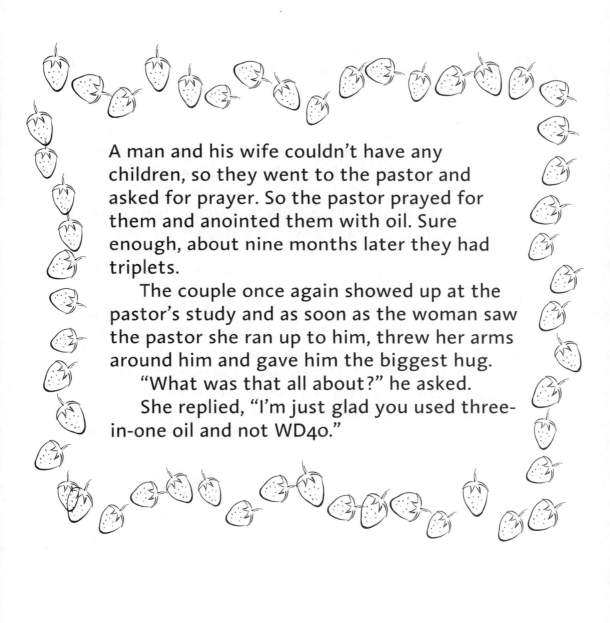

A man and his wife couldn't have any children, so they went to the pastor and asked for prayer. So the pastor prayed for them and anointed them with oil. Sure enough, about nine months later they had triplets.

The couple once again showed up at the pastor's study and as soon as the woman saw the pastor she ran up to him, threw her arms around him and gave him the biggest hug.

"What was that all about?" he asked.

She replied, "I'm just glad you used three-in-one oil and not WD40."

Miracles

A man was driving along the highway and saw a rabbit hopping across the middle of the road. He swerved to avoid hitting it, but unfortunately the rabbit jumped in front of the car and was hit. The driver, being a sensitive man as well as an animal lover, pulled over to the side of the road and got out to see what had become of the rabbit. Much to his dismay, the rabbit was dead. The driver felt so awful that he began to cry.

A woman driving down the highway saw the man crying on the side of the road and pulled over. She stepped out of her car and asked the man what was wrong.

"I feel terrible," he explained. "I accidentally hit this rabbit and killed it."

The woman told the man not to worry. She knew what to do. She went to her car trunk and pulled out a spray can. She walked over to the limp, dead rabbit, and sprayed the contents of the can onto the rabbit. Miraculously, the rabbit came to life, jumped up, waved its paw at the two people and hopped down the road. Ten feet away the rabbit stopped, turned around, waved at the two people again, hopped down the road another ten feet, turned, waved, and hopped another ten feet, turned and waved and repeated this again and again until it was out of sight.

The man was astonished. He couldn't figure out what substance could be in the woman's spray can! He ran over to her and demanded, "What was in your spray can? What did you spray onto that rabbit?"

The woman turned the can around so that the man could read the label.

It said: "Hair Spray — Restores Life to Dead Hair. Adds Permanent Wave."

Misconceptions

During the Second World War, a baby boy was born to a woman whose husband had been called up. He did not see his dad for three years. His mother tried to ease this loss with a little ritual every bedtime. Every night, after putting on his pyjamas, the boy would say his prayers, and then kiss the picture of his dad goodnight, before tumbling into bed.

This went on for three years. Then came the great day when dad returned home. That night dad joined in the bedside ritual. Mum said, "Now you can kiss your father good night". The boy ran over to the picture, kissed the photo, then jumped into bed — leaving his dad standing with open but empty arms.

Mistakes

Mistakes are...

M essages that give us feedback about life.
I nterruptions that should cause us to reflect and think.
S ignposts that direct us to the right path.
T ests that push us towards greater maturity.
A wakenings that keep us in the game mentally.
K eys that we can use to unlock the next door of opportunity.
E xplorations that let us journey where we've never been before.
S tatements about our development and progress

John C Maxwell

"Never confuse a single mistake with a final mistake."
F Scott Fitzgerald

It doesn't matter how much milk you spill, so long as you don't lose the cow.

God has a big eraser.

"If only one could have two lives: the first in which to make one's mistakes, the second in which to profit by them."
D H Lawrence

"If I wasn't making mistakes, I wasn't making decisions."
Robert W Johnson

Try to fix the mistake, not the blame.

Learn from the mistakes of others. You can never live long enough to make them all yourself.

Money

A little boy wanted £100 badly and prayed for one week but nothing happened. Then he decided to write God a letter requesting £100. When the postal authorities received the letter addressed to GOD UK, they decided to send it to the Prime Minister.

The Prime Minister was so impressed, touched, and amused that he instructed his secretary to send the little boy a £5 note. The Prime Minister thought this would appear to be a lot of money to a little boy.

The boy was delighted with the £5 and sat down to write a thank you note to God, which read:

Dear God,

Thank you very much for sending the money. However, I noticed that for some reason you had to send it through 10 Downing Street and, as usual, they took most of it.

Mothers

One mother can take care of five children,
but five children cannot take care of one mother.

Motherhood. A bond that forms before birth,
endures beyond death and shapes us in life even in its absence.

Motherhood, for better or for worse, is life's original influence. Eighty-year-old US Senator Robert Byrd was less than a year old when his mother died. He spoke of her when addressing the Senate in 1998.

"In the one photograph which I have of her, gazing back at me is a blue-eyed, fair-complexioned, pretty young woman with a serious, yet sweet expression and a large bow in her hair. How I wish that I had known her even for one day."

"All that I am or ever hope to be, I owe to my angel Mother."
Abraham Lincoln (1809–1865)

"God could not be everywhere and therefore he made mothers."
Jewish proverb

"Of all the rights of women, the greatest is to be a mother."
Lin Yutang

"The heart of a mother is a deep abyss at the bottom of which you will always find forgiveness."
Honoré de Balzac (1799–1850)

"I remember my mother's prayers and they have always followed me. They have clung to me all my life."
Abraham Lincoln

"Youth fades; love droops, the leaves of friendship fall; A mother's secret hope outlives them all."
Oliver Wendell Holmes
(1809–1894)

"My mother was the most beautiful woman I ever saw. All I am I owe to my mother. I attribute all my success in life to the moral, intellectual and physical education I received from her."
George Washington (1732–1799)

"The mother's heart is the child's schoolroom."
Henry Ward Beecher
(1813–1887)

"By and large, mothers and housewives are the only workers who do not have regular time off. They are the great vacationless class."
Anne Morrow Lindbergh

"The most important thing a father can do for his children is to love their mother."
Walter Trobisch

The joy of motherhood: What a woman experiences when all the children are finally in bed.

"A mother is the truest friend we have, when trials, heavy and sudden, fall upon us; when adversity takes the place of prosperity; when friends who rejoice with us in our sunshine, desert us when troubles thicken around us, still will she cling to us, and endeavour by her kind precepts and counsels to dissipate the clouds of darkness, and cause peace to return to our hearts."
Washington Irving (1783–1859)

Music

"Music is a moral law. It gives soul to the universe, wings to the mind, flight to the imagination, and charm and joy to life and to everything."
Plato

"Without music, life would be an error. The German imagines even God singing songs."
Nietzsche

"I think music in itself is healing. It's an explosive expression of humanity. It's something we are all touched by. No matter what culture we're from, everyone loves music."
Billy Joel

"Opera is when a man gets stabbed in the back and still sings."
Ed Gardner

"To those who understand music, they know that music does not come from your mouth. The only reason that it comes out there is that it has to get out from somewhere. Anyway, music is sung by your heart and your soul, and it is felt by all those who really understand and love it."
A homeless man, interviewed in a night shelter

"If music could be translated into human speech it would no longer need to exist."

Ned Rorem

"Music must rank as the highest of the fine arts — as the one which, more than any other, ministers to human welfare."

Herbert Spencer

"If I don't practice one day, I know it; two days, the critics know it; three days, the public knows it."

Jascha Heifetz

"The one true comment on a piece of music is another piece of music."

Stravinsky

When the orchestra started playing Tchaikovsky's "Romeo and Juliet" overture, a woman noticed tears beginning to run down the cheeks of the elderly man she was seated next to. Before long he was sobbing outright, so she turned and said gently, "You must be an incurable romantic".

"Not at all," he gulped, "I'm a musician."

The great pianist Liszt was asked by Nicholas I of Russia to perform at court. Right in the middle of his first sonata, however, Liszt noticed that the Czar was talking to an aide. Irritated, he continued to play, but when Nicholas continued to converse, the composer finally put his hands in his lap.

The Czar swiftly sent an aide to inquire as to the reason for the interruption.

"When the Czar speaks, everyone should be silent," said Liszt.

There were no further interruptions.

Names

The gospel message was hidden in the names of the first ten generations of humankind — God's provision for us from the beginning of history:

ADAM	means	Man
SETH		(is) appointed
ENOSH		mortal
KENAN		sorrow;
MAHALALEEL		(but) the Blessed God
JARED		shall come down
ENOCH		teaching (that)
METHUSELAH		His death shall bring
LAMECH		(the) despairing
NOAH		rest.

Negotiation

Don't win a battle and lose the war.

"You cannot shake hands with a clenched fist."
Golda Meir (1898–1978), Prime Minister of Israel

"It is better to lose the saddle than the horse."
Italian proverb

"Let us never negotiate out of fear, but let us never fear to negotiate."
John F Kennedy

Noah

Lessons from his life:

1. Don't miss the boat.
2. Remember that we are all in the same boat.
3. Plan ahead. It wasn't raining when Noah built the ark.
4. Stay fit. When you're 600 years old, someone may ask you to do something really big.
5. Don't listen to critics; just get on with the job that needs to be done.
6. Build your future on high ground.
7. For safety's sake, travel in pairs.
8. Speed isn't always an advantage. The snails were on board with the cheetahs.
9. When you're stressed, float a while.
10. No matter the storm, when you are with God, there's always a rainbow waiting.

Obedience

Learn to obey before you command.

Greek proverb

Opinions

Some people fall for everything and stand for nothing.

"If you must tell me your opinions, tell me what you believe in. I have plenty of doubt of my own."

Goethe

Opportunity

The only difference between stumbling blocks and stepping stones is the way you use them.

"Opportunity is missed by most people because it is dressed in overalls and looks like work."

Thomas Edison

In the fields of opportunity it's always ploughing time.

"Gentlemen, we are surrounded by insurmountable opportunities."

Pogo

"When one door closes, another opens; but we often look so long and so regretfully upon the closed door that we do not see the one which has opened for us."

Alexander Graham Bell

Organists

The minister was preoccupied with thoughts of how, after the service, he was going to ask the congregation to come up with more money than they were expecting for repairs to the church building. Therefore, he was annoyed to find that the regular organist was sick and a substitute had been brought in at the last minute. The substitute wanted to know what to play.

"Here's a copy of the service," the minister said impatiently. "But you'll have to think of something to play after I make the announcement about the finances."

During the service, the minister paused and said, "Brothers and sisters, we are in great difficulty; the roof repairs cost twice as much as we expected, and we need £4,000 more. Any of you who can pledge £100 or more, please stand up."

At that moment, the substitute organist played the national anthem.

And that is how the substitute became the regular organist!

P

Packaging

A young man was getting ready to graduate from college. For many months he had admired a beautiful sports car in a dealer's showroom, and knowing his father could well afford it, he told him that he really wanted it.

As graduation day approached, the young man looked for signs that his father had bought the car. Finally, on the morning of his graduation, his father called him into his private study. His father told him how proud he was to have such a fine son, and told him how much he loved him.

He handed his son a beautifully wrapped gift box. Curious, but somewhat disappointed, the young man opened the box and found a lovely leather-bound Bible, with his name embossed in gold.

Angrily, he raised his voice to his father and said, "With all your money you give me a Bible?" and stormed out of the house, leaving the Bible behind.

Many years passed and the young man was very successful in business. He had a beautiful home and wonderful family, but he had not seen his father since graduation day. His father was now very old, and the son thought that perhaps it was time he went to visit him.

Before he could make arrangements, however, he received a telegraph telling him his father had passed away, and willed all his possessions to his son. He needed to come home immediately and take care of things.

When he arrived at his father's house, sudden sadness and regret filled his heart. He began to search through his father's important papers and saw the still-new Bible, just as he had left it years ago.

In tears, he opened the Bible and began to turn the pages. His father had carefully underlined a verse, Matthew 7:11, "If you, though you are evil, know how to give good gifts to your children, how much more will your father in heaven, give to those who ask Him?"

As he read those words, a car key dropped from the back of the Bible. It had a tag with the dealer's name; the same dealer who had the sports car he had desired.

On the tag was the date of his graduation, and the words...PAID IN FULL.

Paradoxes

A true believer is:

Strong enough to be weak
Successful enough to fail
Wise enough to say "I don't know"
Serious enough to laugh
Rich enough to be poor
Right enough to say "I'm wrong"
Mature enough to be childlike
Planned enough to be spontaneous
Controlled enough to be flexible
Free enough to endure captivity
Knowledgeable enough to ask questions
Loving enough to be angry
Great enough to be anonymous
Responsible enough to play
Assured enough to be rejected
Stable enough to cry
Victorious enough to lose.

Parenting

"When I was 14 my father was so ignorant I could hardly bear him, but by the time I was 21 I was amazed to see how much he had learned in the last seven years."

Mark Twain

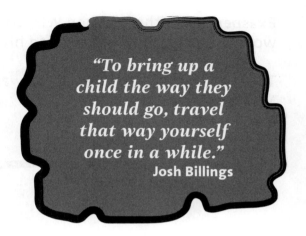

"To bring up a child the way they should go, travel that way yourself once in a while."
Josh Billings

An old country doctor went way out to the boondocks to deliver a baby. It was so far out, there was no electricity. When the doctor arrived, no one was home except for the labouring mother and her five-year-old child.

The doctor instructed the child to hold a lantern high so he could see, while he helped the woman deliver the baby. The child did so, the mother pushed and after a little while, the doctor lifted the newborn baby by the feet and spanked him on the bottom to get him to take his first breath. The doctor then asked the five-year-old what he thought of the baby.

"Hit him again," the five-year-old said. "He shouldn't have crawled up there in the first place!"

Exasperated father: "When Winston Churchill was your age he worked hard all day and studied his books at night."

Teenage son: "Yes, and when he was your age he was Prime Minister."

In loco parentis = Latin for "children drive their parents crazy".

Parenthood has two stages: when your children ask all the questions, and when they think they know all the answers.

Passion

A W Tozer wrote this in the late 1950s, just before the outbreak of the Charismatic Renewal:

"Within the fold of conservative Christianity there are to be found increasing numbers of persons whose religious lives are marked by a growing hunger after God Himself. They are eager for spiritual realities and will not be put off with words, nor will they be content with current interpretations of truth. They are athirst for God, and they will not be satisfied till they have drunk deep at the fountain of Living Water."

Paths

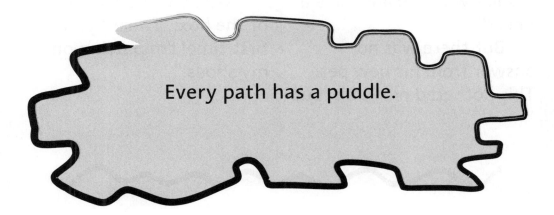

Every path has a puddle.

Patience

A lonely man decided life would be more fun if he had a pet. So he went to the pet store and told the owner that he wanted to buy an unusual pet. After some discussion, he finally bought a centipede, which came in a little white box.

He took the box home, found a good location for it, and decided he would start off by taking his new pet to the bar to have a drink. So he asked the centipede in the box, "Would you like to go to Frank's with me and have a beer?"

But there was no answer from his new pet. This bothered him a bit, but he waited a few minutes and then asked him again, "How about going to the bar and having a drink with me?"

But again, there was no answer from his new friend and pet. He waited a few minutes more, thinking about the situation, and decided to ask him one more time… this time putting his face up against the centipede's house and shouting, "Hey, in there! Would you like to go to Frank's place and have a drink with me?"

A little voice came out of the box: "I heard you the first time! I'm putting on my shoes."

People

> *People want the front of the bus, back of the church and centre of attention.*

Perseverance

"Ride on, ride on! Rough-shod if need be;
Smooth-shod if that will do, but ride on!
Ride over all obstacles, and win the race!"
Charles Dickens

"It is a long road
from conception to
completion."
Molière

"Victory belongs
to the most
persevering."
Napoleon Bonaparte

George Friedrich Handel was a failure. Bankrupted, in great physical pain, and the victim of plots to sabotage his career, the once-great composer scheduled a "farewell" appearance in London in April 1741. To the London élite, it looked like this "German nincompoop", as he was once called, was through. That summer, however, he composed the *Messiah*, which not only brought him back into the spotlight but is still deemed by some to be "an epitome of Christian faith".

Discouragement came early. His father wanted him to be a lawyer, not a musician. Even after he was able to take up a musical career (becoming the composer for England's Chapel Royal), he preferred the out-of-fashion operas to the more popular music of the day — which often meant playing to empty halls. (Never mind, he joked, an empty venue would mean great acoustics.)

He didn't joke for long. In 1737 Handel's opera company went bankrupt, and he suffered what seems to have been a mild stroke. But to make matters worse, his latest musical fascination — the oratorio (a composition for orchestra and voices telling a sacred story without costumes, scenery, or dramatic action) was his most controversial yet. His first oratorio (actually, the first of its kind in English), *Esther*, was met with outrage by the church. A Bible story was being told by "common mummers", and even worse, the words of God were being spoken in the theater!

In 1739, advertisements for *Israel in Egypt* were torn down by devout Christians, who also disrupted its performances. All of this angered the devoutly Lutheran Handel. As his friend Sir John Hawkins commented, "Throughout his life, [he] manifested a deep sense of religion. In conversation he would frequently declare the pleasure he felt in setting the Scriptures to music, and how contemplating the many sublime passages in the Psalms had contributed to his edification."

Deeply depressed and now threatened with debtor's prison, Handel was visited by his friend Charles Jennens, who had written a libretto about the life of Christ with the text completely taken from the Bible. Would Handel compose the music for it? he asked. Handel answered that he would and estimated its completion in a year.

Handel began composing the *Messiah* on 22 August 1741, and worked like a man obsessed. He rarely left his room and rarely touched his meals. But in 24 days he had composed 260 pages — an immense physical feat. When he finished writing what would become known as the Hallelujah Chorus, he said, "I did think I did see all Heaven before me, and the great God himself."

Though the performance of the piece again caused controversy (Jonathan Swift, author of *Gulliver's Travels* and then the dean of Saint Patrick's Cathedral, was outraged and initially refused to allow his musicians to participate), the première, a benefit performance on 13 April 1742, at Dublin's Fishamble Street Musick Hall, was a sensation.

Still it took nearly a year for *Messiah* to be invited to London. Religious controversy surrounded it there, too, and Handel compromised a bit by dropping the "blasphemous" title from handbills. It was instead called "A New Sacred Oratorio". But the controversy wasn't strong enough to keep away the king, who stood instantly at the opening notes of the Hallelujah Chorus (though some historians have suggested it was because he was partially deaf and mistook it for the national anthem), a tradition ever since.

Though it had met rave reviews in Dublin ("the most finished piece of music"), it was not very popular in London after its première. By 1745 Handel was again playing to empty houses and close to poverty. Not until his oratorio *Judas Maccabeus*, which was misunderstood by the English as a veiled nationalistic anthem, did Handel (and with him *Messiah*) reach the pinnacle of his career.

Until his death, Handel conducted 30 performances of *Messiah* (none at Christmastime, for Handel deemed it a Lenten piece), only one of which was in a church, Bristol Cathedral. In that audience sat John Wesley. "I doubt if that congregation was ever so serious at a sermon as they were during this performance," the founder of Methodism remarked.

The late Earl Nightingale, writer and publisher of inspirational and motivational material, once told a story about a boy named Sparky. For Sparky, school was all but impossible. He failed every subject in the eighth grade. He flunked physics in high school, getting a grade of zero.

Sparky also flunked Latin, algebra, and English. He didn't do much better in sports. Although he did manage to make the school's golf team, he promptly lost the only important match of the season. There was a consolation match; he lost that too.

Throughout his youth, Sparky was awkward socially. He was not actually disliked by the other students; no one cared that much. He was astonished if a classmate ever said hello to him outside of school hours. There's no way to tell how he might have done at dating. Sparky never once asked a girl to go out in high school. He was too afraid of being turned down.

Sparky was a loser. He, his classmates, everyone knew it. So he rolled with it. Sparky had made up his mind early in life that if things were meant to work out, they would. Otherwise he would content himself with what appeared to be his inevitable mediocrity. However, one thing was important to Sparky — drawing. He was proud of his artwork. Of course, no one else appreciated it. In his senior year of high school, he submitted some cartoons to the editors of the yearbook. The cartoons were turned down. Despite this particular rejection, Sparky was so convinced of his ability that he decided to become a professional artist.

After completing high school, he wrote a letter to Walt Disney Studios. He was told to send some samples of his artwork, and the subject for a cartoon was suggested. Sparky drew the proposed cartoon. He spent a great deal of time on it and on all the other drawings he submitted. Finally, the reply came from Disney Studios. He had been rejected once again. Another loss for the loser.

So Sparky decided to write his own autobiography in cartoons. He described his childhood self — a little boy loser and chronic underachiever. The cartoon character would soon become famous worldwide.

For Sparky, the boy who had such lack of success in school and whose work was rejected again and again, was Charles Schulz. He created the "Peanuts" comic strip and the little cartoon character whose kite would never fly and who never succeeded in kicking a football — Charlie Brown.

Perspective

If we could shrink the Earth's population to a village of precisely 100 people, with all the existing human ratios remaining the same, it would look something like the following:

There would be:

57 Asians
21 Europeans
14 from the Western Hemisphere, both north and south
8 Africans

52 would be female
48 would be male

70 would be non-white
30 would be white

70 would be non-Christian
30 would be Christian

6 people would possess 59% of the entire world's wealth and all 6 would be from the United States
80 would live in substandard housing
70 would be unable to read
50 would suffer from malnutrition
1 would be near death
1 would be near birth
1 (yes, only 1) would have a college education
1 would own a computer.

Memo From God

Reference: LIFE

I am God. Today I will be handling all of your problems. Please remember that I do not need your help.

If life happens to deliver a situation to you that you cannot handle, do not attempt to resolve it. Kindly put it in the SFGTD (something for God to do) box. It will be addressed in My time, not yours. Once the matter is placed into the box, do not hold onto it.

If you find yourself stuck in traffic, don't despair. There are people in this world for whom driving is an unheard-of privilege.

Should you have a bad day at work, think of the man who has been out of work for years.

Should you despair over a relationship gone bad, think of the person who has never known what it's like to love and be loved in return.

Should you grieve the passing of another weekend, think of the woman in dire straits, working twelve hours a day, seven days a week to feed her children.

Should your car break down, leaving you miles away from assistance, think of the paraplegic who would love the opportunity to take that walk.

Should you notice a new grey hair in the mirror, think of the cancer patient in chemotherapy who wishes she had hair to examine.

Should you find yourself at a loss and pondering what is life all about, asking what is my purpose? Be thankful. There are those who didn't live long enough to get the opportunity.

Should you find yourself the victim of other people's bitterness, ignorance, smallness or insecurities, remember, things could be worse. You could be them!

Always remember. . . "The greatest oak was once a little nut that held its ground."

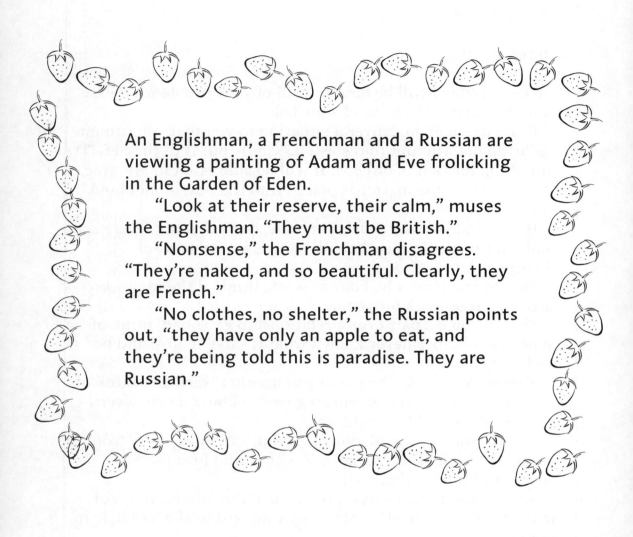

An Englishman, a Frenchman and a Russian are viewing a painting of Adam and Eve frolicking in the Garden of Eden.

"Look at their reserve, their calm," muses the Englishman. "They must be British."

"Nonsense," the Frenchman disagrees. "They're naked, and so beautiful. Clearly, they are French."

"No clothes, no shelter," the Russian points out, "they have only an apple to eat, and they're being told this is paradise. They are Russian."

Phones

A group of men are sitting in a sauna discussing business and stocks when suddenly a cellular phone rings.

"Hi honey, are you at the club?"

"Yes, dear."

"Honey you won't believe this but I'm standing in front of Giovannis and there's a beautiful mink on sale in the window."

"How much is it, dear?"

"They're giving it away. Only $5,000. Can you believe it?"

"But you already have fur coats."

"Please dear, it's absolutely exquisite!"

"Fine, fine go ahead and buy it!"

"Thank you sweetheart. Oh, not to keep you much longer, I passed by the Mercedes dealership this morning and saw their new convertible. It was to die for! I talked to the salesman and the one in the showroom is brand new, leather seats, power everything, gold coloured. What do you think?"

"Honey, come on, we already have cars!"

"You promised me that I could get a convertible!"

"How much is it?"

"You won't believe it but he said he'd let us have it for $85,000 fully loaded with all the options!"

"OK, OK, go ahead and purchase it!"

"I love you, you're the best husband a wife could ask for. I hope I'm not pushing it, but remember the trip we took to Paris? Remember the Brown's place with the swimming pool, tennis courts? It's on the market. I saw it this morning at the real estate agency. If we bought it we would have a perfect place to stay during the cold winter months!"

"I had actually thought about it. You say it's on the market?"

"Really, you were actually thinking about it? Can I go make an offer on it? You know it's not listed very high, and it would be perfect for our type of lifestyle!"

"How much is it listed at?"

"Only $425,000 sweetheart. It's a steal!"

"I guess we've got money put away. Go ahead and make an offer but no more than $415,000."

"This is turning out to be a great day! Can't wait to see you later tonight to celebrate!"

"See you tonight dear."

The man puts down the cellular phone and asks, "So, whose phone is this?"

Planning

When you fail to plan, you plan to fail.

Plan ahead. It wasn't raining when Noah built the ark.

*"God has no problems,
only plans."*
Corrie Ten Boom

Politics

Pure socialism: You have two cows. The government takes them and puts them in a barn with everyone else's cows. You have to take care of all the cows. The government gives you as much milk as you need.

Fascism: You have two cows. The government takes both, hires you to take care of them, and sells you the milk.

Pure communism: You have two cows. Your neighbours help you take care of them, and you all share the milk.

Dictatorship: You have two cows. The government takes both and shoots you.

Militarism: You have two cows. The government takes both and drafts you.

Pure democracy: You have two cows. Your neighbours decide who gets the milk.

British democracy: You have two cows. You feed them sheep's brains and they go mad. The government doesn't do anything.

European bureaucracy: You have two cows. At first the government regulates what you can feed them and when you can milk them. Then it pays you not to milk them. After that it takes both, shoots one, milks the other and pours the milk down the drain. Then it requires you to fill out forms accounting for the missing cows.

Anarchy: You have two cows. Either you sell the milk at a fair price or your neighbours try to kill you and take the cows.

Capitalism: You have two cows. You sell one and buy a bull.

Environmentalism: You have two cows. The government bans you from milking or killing them.

Feminism: You have two cows. They get married and adopt a veal calf.

Totalitarianism: You have two cows. The government takes them and denies they ever existed. Milk is banned.

Political correctness: You are associated with (the concept of "ownership" is a symbol of the masculine, war-mongering, intolerant past) two differently-aged (but no less valuable to society) bovines of non-specified gender.

Counter culture: Wow, dude, there's like…these two cows, man. You got to have some of this milk.

Surrealism: You have two giraffes. The government requires you to take harmonica lessons.

Potential

"My mother said to me, 'If you become a soldier, you'll be a general; if you become a monk, you'll end up as a Pope.' Instead I became a painter and wound up as Picasso."
Pablo Picasso (1881–1973)

Life is like a 15-speed bike. Most of us have gears we never use.

Prayer

Scientists in New York have found that prayer doubled the chances of successful IVF treatment in a study. The Columbia University team say a group who had people praying for them had a 50% pregnancy rate compared to a 26% rate in others. The researchers admit the results seem incredible, but say unknown biological factors may be causing the differences. They are certain the study was error-proof because the women who took part didn't even know they were being prayed for.

A total of 100 women were randomly assigned to a prayer group and 99 others to a non-prayer group. The prayer group was given pictures of the prospective mothers, but the women being prayed for didn't even know of the group's existence. Dr Rogerio Lobo, from Columbia University College of Physicians & Surgeons, carried out the study in Seoul, South Korea, and published it in the *Journal of Reproductive Medicine*.

He said: "We could have ignored the findings, but that would not help to advance the field." He added, "We are putting the results out there hoping to provoke discussion and see if anything can be learned from it. We would like to understand the biological or other phenomena that led to this almost doubling of the pregnancy rate."

Patients admitted to hospital with heart problems suffer fewer complications if someone prays for them, according to scientists in the US. The study, carried out at Duke University Medical Center in North Carolina, found that patients who received alternative therapy following angioplasty were 25% to 30% less likely to suffer complications. And those who received "intercessory prayer" had the greatest success rate. The study, carried out between April 1997 and April 1998, involved 150 patients who had all undergone angioplasty — whereby a balloon is positioned in a hardened and narrowed artery and inflated to force it open. This procedure was followed in all cases by coronary artery stenting — which involves a flexible mesh tube being inserted into the artery to keep it open.

Patients were chosen randomly to receive coronary stenting with standard care or coronary stenting plus one of four alternative therapies — guided imagery, stress relaxation, healing touch or intercessory prayer.

Intercessory prayer was provided by seven prayer groups of varying denominations around the world. Neither the researchers nor the patients were aware who was being prayed for but the results showed that, of all the therapies, prayer appeared to have the greatest therapeutic benefits.

Suzanne Crater, a nurse practitioner and co-director of the study, said the clinical outcomes between treatment groups were not significantly different but those receiving alternative therapies "had lower absolute complication rates and a lower absolute incidence of post-procedural ischemia during hospitalization". Complications after angioplasty include death, heart failure, post-procedural ischemia, repeat angioplasty or heart attack.

Dr Harold Koenig, associate professor of psychiatry at Duke University Medical Center, said: "*Some of the greatest scientific achievements have come from those who step outside of the box* and I believe that is what this study does. The results tend to lean toward prayer helping people but more study is needed."

The small ship was weathering a terrible storm and taking on water. After a time, the pumps broke down, and the vessel began to sink. The crew quickly herded the passengers into the lifeboats. While all this was going on, the captain called out, "Does anyone here know how to pray?"

A humble clergyman stepped forward. "I can pray," he said softly.

Just then, a rival minister jumped up. "I think I would do a better job!" he declared outright. "You're so quiet that your prayer can't even be heard across a quiet church, much less a noisy storm."

"Very well," the captain said, pointing to the second, boastful minister. "You pray — we're short one life jacket."

A woman was at work when she received a phone call telling her that her daughter was ill. She left work and went to the pharmacist to buy some flu medicine. Unfortunately, having done so, she returned to discover she'd locked her keys in the car.

She looked around for a rusty coat hanger, found one, but didn't know how to use it. So she bowed her head and prayed for help. Within seconds a scruffy man appeared. She was so desperate she told him her plight and asked him, "Do you know how to break into a car with one of these?"

"Sure," said the man, and within a minute had opened the car door.

The woman hugged him and thanked him profusely. "Thank you so much," she said, "You are a very nice man."

The man replied, "Lady, I am not a nice man. I just got out of prison today. I was in prison for car theft and have only been out for one hour."

"Thank you, Lord," shouted the woman, "for sending me a professional!"

Open my eyes that I may see
 the Presence that is all about me.
Open my ears that I may hear
 the voice that is quiet yet ever near.
Open my heart that I may feel
 the love of God close and real.
Open each sense, make me aware of the
 Power and Peace always there.

> *"I have lived to thank God that not all my prayers have been answered."*
> **Jean Ingelow**

A minister parked his car in a no-parking zone in a large city because he was short of time and couldn't find a space with a meter. So he put a note under the windshield wiper that read: I have circled the block 10 times. If I don't park here, I'll miss my appointment. FORGIVE US OUR TRESPASSES.

When he returned, he found a citation from a police officer along with this note. I've circled this block for 10 years. If I don't give you a ticket, I'll lose my job. LEAD US NOT INTO TEMPTATION.

"Prayer does not change God, but it changes those who pray."
Soren Kierkegaard

Preachers

A rich man went to his vicar and said, "I want you and your wife to take a three-month trip to the Holy Land at my expense. When you come back, I'll have a surprise for you." The vicar accepted the offer and he and his wife went off to the Middle East.

Three months later they returned home and were met by the wealthy parishioner, who told them while they were gone, he had had a new church built. "It's the finest building money can buy, Vicar," said the man, "No expense was spared." And he was right. It was a magnificent building both outside and in.

But there was one striking difference. There was only one pew and it was at the very back. "A church with only one pew?" asked the vicar.

"You just wait until Sunday," said the rich man.

When the time came for the Sunday service, the early arrivals entered the church, filed onto the one pew and sat down. When the pew was full, a switch clicked silently, a circuit closed, the gears meshed, a belt moved and, automatically, the rear pew began to move forward. When it reached the front of the church it came to a stop. At the same time, another empty pew came up from below at the back and more people sat down. And so it continued, pews filling and moving forwards until finally the church was full, from front to back.

"Wonderful!" said the vicar, "Marvelous!"

The service began, and the vicar started to preach his sermon. He launched into his text and, when 12 o'clock came, he was still going strong with no end in sight. Suddenly a bell rang and a trap door in the floor behind the pulpit dropped open.

"Wonderful!" said the congregation, "Marvelous!"

Preaching

The minister just had all of his remaining teeth pulled out and new dentures were being made.

The first Sunday, he only preached ten minutes. The second Sunday, he preached only 20 minutes. But, on the third Sunday he preached 1 hour 25 minutes.

When asked about this by some of the congregation, he responded this way: "The first Sunday, my gums were so sore it hurt to talk. The second Sunday, my dentures were hurting a lot. The third Sunday, I accidentally grabbed my wife's dentures and I could not stop talking!"

A good example is the best sermon.

Problems

For every problem
Under the sun
There is a solution
Or there is none.
If there's a solution
Go and find it.
If there isn't
Never mind it.

Protection

An article in *National Geographic* several years ago provided a penetrating picture of God's wings.

After a forest fire in Yellowstone National Park, forest rangers began their trek up a mountain to assess the inferno's damage. One ranger found a bird literally petrified in ashes, perched statuesquely on the ground at the base of a tree. Somewhat sickened by the eerie sight, he knocked the bird over with a stick. When he struck it, three tiny chicks scurried from under their dead mother's wings. The loving mother, keenly aware of impending disaster, had carried her offspring to the base of the tree and had gathered them under her wings, instinctively knowing that the toxic smoke would rise.

She could have flown to safety but had refused to abandon her babies. When the blaze had arrived and the heat had scorched her small body, the mother had remained steadfast. Because she had been willing to die, those under the cover of her wings would live.

"He will cover you with his feathers, and under his wings you will find refuge" (Psalm 91:4).

Provision

And it came to pass after these things that God did test Avraham. And God said to him, "Avraham!" And Avraham replied "Hineni — here I am."

And God said, "Take your computer, your old computer, your 286 and install upon it an operating system, a new operating system, Windows 98 which I will show to you."

And Avraham rose up early in the morning, and saddled his ass. He loaded his computer, his old computer, his 286, on the ass. And he took two of his young men with Him and Yitzchak his son. And he rose up and went to the place where God had told him, there to find Windows 98.

Then, on the third day, Avraham lifted his eyes and saw Windows 98 from afar. And Avraham said to his young men, "Stay here with the ass; and I and the lad will go yonder and load Windows 98 on our 286, and come again to you."

And Avraham took his computer his old computer, his 286, and laid it on Yitzchak his son. And they went both of them together. And Yitzchak spoke to Avraham his father and said, "My father".

And he replied, "Hineni — Here I am my son."

And Yitzchak said, "Windows 98 requires far more memory than a 286 has. How will it possibly run on your machine?"

And Avraham looked at his son, his only son, whom he loved; and he shook his head slowly, and in perfect faith and with unswerving trust and belief in the Almighty, he said, "Fear not, Yitzchak my son, God will provide the RAM."

Purpose

A little camel comes to the mommy camel and says, "Mommy, why have I got such big flat feet?" Mommy says, "Well, darling, in the desert you need big flat feet because the sand is soft and they help us to keep stable."

The little camel goes away and then comes back, "Mommy, mommy, why have I got such big eyelashes?" "Well, darling, in the desert when there is a lot of wind the sand gets thrown about in the air and we need big eyelashes to stop the sand getting in our eyes." The little camel goes away.

He comes back and says, "Mommy, mommy, why have I got a hump back?" "Well, darling, out in the desert sometimes we are without water for a long, long time and we have got the hump which is designed to store a lot of water and it helps us to survive in the desert." The camel goes away.

He comes back, "Mommy, mommy, I know we have got big feet and long eyelashes and a hump, but why are we in Bristol Zoo?"

Somebody has well said that there are only two kinds of people in the world: those who wake up in the morning and say, "Good morning, Lord", and those who wake up in the morning and say, "Good Lord, it's morning".

Quakers

A Quaker farmer was milking his cows, and near the end of the milking one of the cows lifted her tail, swished him hard across the face, shifted legs and, with the free leg, kicked both the farmer and the milk pail (nearly full of milk) spilling it into the farmer's shoes.

"Oh, dear cow," said the Quaker, "thou knowest that my pacifism dost not allow me to beat thee, that I canst not even curse thee for these impertinent actions. Thou mayest believe that thou canst escape retribution for this pagan action. And, thou mayest even thinkest thee smarter than myself.

"But what thou knowest not is that I can sell thee to Ole, my Norwegian Lutheran neighbour, who canst beat the living tar out of thee."

Quality

"If you don't do it excellently, don't do it at all."
Robert Townsend

"Quality is not an act, it is a habit."
Aristotle

"It is better to deserve honors and not have them, than to have them and not deserve them."

Mark Twain

Sign in a restaurant window,
"Courteous and efficient
self-service".

A man ordered breakfast in a hotel: "I want two eggs, one of them runny as water and the other cooked hard enough to bounce. I want the toast burned black, the coffee cold, and the butter too hard to cut."

"We can't do that, sir," protested the waitress.

"Sure you can," said the man, "You did it perfectly well yesterday."

Questions

"It is not every question that deserves an answer."
Publius Syrus

"It is easier to judge a person's mental capacity by their questions than by their answers."
De Luc de Levis

1. Why is the third hand on the watch called the second hand?
2. If a word is misspelled in the dictionary, how would we ever know?
3. If Webster wrote the first dictionary, where did he find the words?
4. Why do we say something is out of whack? What is a whack?
5. Why do "slow down" and "slow up" mean the same thing?
6. Why do "fat chance" and "slim chance" mean the same thing?
7. Why do "tug" boats push their barges?
8. Why are they called "stands" when they are made for sitting?
9. Why is it called "after dark" when it really is "after light"?
10. Doesn't "expecting the unexpected" make the unexpected expected?
11. Why are a "wise man" and a "wise guy" opposites?
12. Why do "overlook" and "oversee" mean opposite things?
13. Why is "phonics" not spelled the way it sounds?
14. If work is so terrific, why do they have to pay you to do it?
15. If all the world is a stage, where is the audience sitting?
16. If love is blind, why is lingerie so popular?
17. Why do you press harder on the buttons of a remote control when you know the batteries are dead?
18. Why do we put suits in garment bags and garments in a suitcase?
19. How come abbreviated is such a long word?
20. Why do we wash bath towels? Aren't we clean when we use them?
21. Why doesn't glue stick to the inside of the bottle?
22. Why do they call it a TV set when you only have one?

Quotations

> "Quotations, when engraved upon the memory,
> give you good thoughts."
>
> **Winston Churchill**

> *"Next to the originator of a good sentence is the first quoter of it."*
>
> **R W Emerson**

> *"I quote others only the better to express myself."*
>
> **Michel de Montaigne**

Quotes

A good sermon should have a good beginning and a good ending, and they should be as close together as possible.

Puritanism: The haunting fear that someone, somewhere, may be happy.

I am an agnostic pagan. I doubt the existence of many gods.

"I don't question YOUR existence."

God

Adam to Eve: I'll wear the plants in this family!

The Bible tells us to love our neighbours, and also to love our enemies, probably because they are generally the same people.

The lion and the calf shall lie down together but the calf won't get much sleep.

On the sixth day, God created the platypus. And God said: "Let's see the evolutionists try and figure this one out."

If you ever think you are too small to be effective, you've never been in bed with a mosquito.

Most people use their hands and feet to drive — a few also use their heads.

To handle yourself, use your head; to handle others, use your heart.

Anger is only one letter short of danger.

Great minds discuss ideas; average minds discuss events; small minds discuss people.

He who loses money, loses much; he who loses a friend, loses much more; he who loses faith, loses all.

Many people will walk in and out of your life, but only true friends will leave footprints in your heart.

Beautiful young people are accidents of nature, but beautiful old people are works of art.

R

Radical

> *A radical is anyone whose opinions differ radically from mine.*

Readiness

> Allstate Insurance Company recently surveyed Californians in earthquake-prone regions. Sixty-four per cent of respondents believe a massive earthquake will hit in three to five years; but only one in four has earthquake insurance.

Refining

Some women met to study the Bible. While reading the third chapter of Malachi, they came upon a remarkable expression in the third verse: "He will sit as a refiner and purifier of silver" (Malachi 3:3).

One lady decided to visit a silversmith, and report to the others on what he said about the subject. She went accordingly, and without telling him the reason for her visit, begged the silversmith to tell her about the process of refining silver.

After he had fully described it to her, she asked, "Sir, do you sit while the work of refining is going on?" "Oh, yes ma'am," replied the silversmith, "I must sit and watch the furnace constantly, for, if the time necessary for refining is exceeded in the slightest degree, the silver will be injured."

The lady at once saw the beauty and comfort of the expression, "He shall sit as a refiner and purifier of silver." God sees it necessary to put His children into the furnace; but His eye is steadily intent on the work of purifying, and His wisdom and love are both engaged in the best manner for us. Our trials do not come at random, and He will not let us be tested beyond what we can endure.

Before she left, the lady asked one final question, "How do you know when the process is complete?" "That's quite simple," replied the silversmith. "When I can see my own image in the silver, the refining process is complete."

Reflections

1. I'm not into working out. My philosophy is no pain, no pain.
2. I'm in shape. Round is a shape.
3. I've always wanted to be somebody, but I should have been more specific.
4. Ever notice when you blow in a dog's face he gets mad at you, but when you take him in a car he sticks his head out the window?
5. Ever notice that anyone driving slower than you is an idiot, but anyone going faster is a maniac?
6. You have to stay in shape. My mother started walking five miles a day when she was 60. She's 97 now and we have no idea where she is.
7. I have six locks on my door, all in a row. When I go out, I lock every other one. I figure no matter how long somebody stands there picking the locks, they are always locking three of them.

Relationships

Something to think about before you take the plunge...

"You got to find somebody who likes the same stuff. Like if you like sports, she should like it that you like sports, and she should keep them chips and dip coming."

Allan, age 10

"No person really decides before they grow up who they're going to marry. God decides it all way before, and you got to find out later who you're stuck with."

Kirsten, age 10

Concerning the proper age to get married:

"Twenty-three is the best age because you know the person FOREVER by then!"

Cam, age 10

"No age is good to get married at... You got to be a fool to get married!"

Freddie, age 6

How can a stranger tell if two people are married?

"Married people usually look happy to talk to other people."

Eddie, age 6

"You might have to guess based on whether they seem to be yelling at the same kids."

Derrick, age 8

What do you think mom and dad have in common?

"Both don't want no more kids."

Lori, age 8

What do most people do on a date?

"Dates are for having fun, and people should use them to get to know each other. Even boys have something to say if you listen long enough."

Lynnette, age 8

"On the first date, they just tell each other lies, and that usually gets them interested enough to go for a second date."

Martin, age 10

What the children would do on a first date that was turning sour?

"I'd run home and play dead. The next day I would call all the newspapers and make sure they wrote about me in all the dead columns."

Craig, age 9

When is it okay to kiss someone?

"When they're rich!"

Pam, age 7

"The law says you have to be 18, so I wouldn't want to mess with that."

Curt, age 7

Better to be single or married?

"It's better for girls to be single but not for boys. Boys need somebody to clean up after them!"

Anita, age 9

"Single is better... for the simple reason that I wouldn't want to change no diapers... Of course, if I did get married, I'd figure something out. I'd just phone my mother and have her come over for some coffee and nappy-changing."

Kirsten, age 10

What advice do you have for a young couple about to be married?

"The first thing I'd say to them is: 'Listen up, youngsters... I got something to say to you. Why in the heck do you wanna get married, anyway?'"

Craig, age 9

What promises do a man and a woman make when they get married?

"A man and a woman promise to go through sickness and illness and diseases together."

Marion, age 10

How to make a marriage work:

"Tell your wife that she looks pretty even if she looks like a truck!"

Ricky, age 7

"If you want to last with your man, you should wear a lot of sexy clothes. Especially underwear that is red and maybe has a few diamonds on it."

Lori, age 8

Religion

"People will wrangle for religion; write for it; fight for it; die for it; anything but live for it."
C C Colton

"Some people have just enough religion to make them uncomfortable."
John Wesley

The worst moment for the atheist is when they are really thankful, and have nobody to thank.

The religion of some people is well developed at the mouth, but lame at the hands and feet.

A religion that costs nothing does nothing.

Revival

Romance

A man is taking a walk and sees a frog on the side of the road. As he comes closer, the frog starts to talk. "Kiss me and I will turn into a princess." The man picks the frog up and puts it in his pocket.

The frog starts shouting, "Hey! Didn't you hear me? I'm a princess. Just kiss me and I will be yours." The man takes the frog out of his pocket and smiles at it and puts it back.

The frog is really frustrated. "I don't get it. Why won't you kiss me? I will turn into a beautiful princess and do anything you ask."

The man says, "Look, I'm a computer geek. I don't have time for girls. But a talking frog is cool!"

You should've listened to me. All those years ago. I tried to tell you. You wouldn't listen...

oh shush

S

Sacrifice

In 1937, a man by the name of John Griffiths found a job tending one of the railroad bridges that crossed the Mississippi River. Every day he would control the gears of the bridge to allow barges and ships through.

One day John decided to allow his eight-year-old son Greg to help him. He and his boy packed their lunches with great excitement and high hopes for the future and went to work. The morning went quickly and at noon they headed off for lunch, down a narrow catwalk onto an observation platform about 50 feet above the Mississippi. John told his son stories about the ships as they passed by.

Suddenly, they were jolted back to reality by the shrill sound of an engine's whistle. Looking at his watch, John realized to his horror that it was 1.07pm, that the Memphis Express was due any time and that the bridge was still raised.

He calmly told Greg to stay put and then ran back to the controls. Once there he looked beneath the bridge to make sure there was nothing below. As his eyes moved downwards he saw something so terrible that he froze. For there, lying on the gears, was his beloved son. Greg had tried to follow his dad but had fallen off the catwalk.

Immediately, John realized the horrifying choice before him: either to lower the bridge and kill his son, or to keep the bridge raised and kill everyone on board the train. As 400 people moved closer to the bridge, John realized what he had to do. Burying his face under his arm, he plunged down the lever. The cries of his son were instantly drowned out by the noise of the bridge grinding slowly into position.

John wiped the tears from his eyes as the train passed by. A conductor was collecting tickets in his usual way. A businessman was casually reading a newspaper. Ladies were drinking afternoon tea. Children were playing. Most of the passengers were engaged in idle chatter. No one saw. No one heard the cries of a heartbroken father.

A pastor in a church in America was about to start his sermon during an evening service when he briefly introduced a visiting minister in the congregation. He said that the visitor was one of his dearest childhood friends and accordingly asked him to say a few words. With that, an elderly man walked to the pulpit and told a story:

"A father, his son, and a friend of his son were sailing off the Pacific coast when a fierce storm hit them and the three were swept into the sea as the boat capsized. Grabbing a rescue line, the father had to make the most painful decision of his life. Who was he to throw the lifeline to? The father knew his own son was a Christian and that the son's friend was not. The father yelled 'I love you' to his boy as he threw the line to the boy's friend, pulling him to safety, while his son disappeared forever beneath the waves. The father knew his son would step into eternity with Jesus but couldn't bear the thought of the friend stepping into an eternity without Jesus. Therefore he sacrificed his son to save the son's friend."

Concluding, the visitor said, "How great is God's love for us that he gave his only Son that we should be rescued. So take hold of the lifeline that the Father is throwing you in this service tonight."

With that the old man finished and the pastor took his place in the pulpit, and preached his message.

At the end of the meeting, some teenagers came up to the visitor. They had been looking very skeptical throughout the old man's story and had not responded to the appeal. "That wasn't a very realistic story," they said mockingly. "No dad would do that."

"You've got a point," said the visitor. "But I'm standing here tonight to tell you that this story gives me personally a great glimpse into the Father's love for us. You see, I was that father, and your pastor here is my son's friend."

Back in the fifteenth century, in a tiny village near Nuremberg, lived a family with 18 children. In order merely to keep food on the table for this mob, the father and head of the household, a goldsmith by profession, worked almost 18 hours a day at his trade and any other paying chore he could find in the neighbourhood.

Despite their seemingly hopeless condition, two of Albrecht Dürer the Elder's children had a dream. They both wanted to pursue their talent for art, but they knew full well that their father would never be financially able to send either of them to Nuremberg to study at the academy.

After many long discussions at night in their crowded bed the two boys finally worked out a pact. They would toss a coin. The loser would go down into the nearby mines and, with his earnings, support his brother while he attended the academy. Then, when the brother who won the toss had completed his studies, in four years, he would support the other brother, either with sales of his artwork or, if necessary, also by labouring in the mines.

They tossed a coin on Sunday morning after church. Albrecht Dürer won the toss and went off to Nuremberg.

Albert went down the dangerous mines and, for the next four years, financed his brother, whose work at the academy was almost an immediate sensation. Albrecht's etchings, his woodcuts, and his oils were far better than those of most of his professors, and by the time he graduated he was beginning to earn considerable fees for his commissioned works.

When the young artist returned to his village, the Dürer family held a festive dinner on their lawn to celebrate Albrecht's triumphant homecoming. After a long and memorable meal, punctuated with music and laughter, Albecht rose from his honoured position at the head of the table to drink a toast to his beloved brother for the years of sacrifice that had enabled Albrecht to fulfil his ambition. His closing words were, "And now, Albert, blessed brother of mine, now it is your turn. Now you can go to Nuremberg to pursue your dream, and I will take care of you."

All heads turned in eager expectation to the far end of the table where Albert sat, tears steaming down his pale face, shaking his lowered head from side to side while he sobbed and repeated, over and over "No… no… no… no."

Finally, Albert rose and wiped

the tears from his cheeks. He glanced down the long table at the faces he loved, and then, holding his hands close to his right cheek, he said softly, "No brother. I cannot go to Nuremberg. It is too late for me. Look…look what four years in the mines have done to my hands! The bones in every finger have been smashed at least once, and lately I have been suffering from arthritis so badly in my right hand that I cannot even hold a glass to return your toast, much less paint delicate lines on parchment or canvas with pen and brush. No, brother…for me it is too late."

More than 450 years have passed. By now, Albrecht Dürer's hundreds of masterful portraits, pen and silver-point sketches, watercolours, charcoals, woodcuts, and copper engravings hang in every great museum in the world, but the odds are great that you, like most people, are familiar with only one of Albrecht Dürer's works. More than merely being familiar with it, you very well may have a reproduction hanging in your home or office.

One day, to pay homage to Albert for all that he had sacrificed, Albrecht Dürer painstakingly drew his brother's abused hands with palms together and thin fingers stretched skyward. He called his powerful drawing simply "Hands", but the entire world almost immediately opened their hearts to his great masterpiece and renamed his tribute of love "The Praying Hands".

Service

"The only ones among you who will be really happy are those who will have sought and found how to serve."
Albert Schweitzer

Sex

When little Susie came home from her first day at school, she promptly asked her mum, "What is sex?"

Susie's mother had been expecting the question for some time, so she launched into a speech about the birds and the bees and eggs and sperm and what happens when two people love each other very much and so on.

Noticing her daughter's brow was still furrowed, she stopped talking.

"Susie, haven't you been able to follow what I've been telling you?"

"I have, Mom, I really have," replied Susie, pulling her school registration card out of her backpack. "But how am I going to fit all that in this little box?"

Sin

"We have a strange illusion that time cancels sins, but mere time does nothing either to the fact or the guilt of sin. The guilt is washed out not by time but by repentance and the blood of Jesus Christ."

C S Lewis

Singing

Chippie the budgie never saw it coming. One second he was peacefully perched in his cage. The next, he was sucked in, washed up and blown over.

The problems began when Chippie's owner decided to clean Chippie's cage with a vacuum cleaner. She removed the attachment from the end of the hose and stuck it in the cage. The phone rang and she turned to pick it up. She'd barely said "Hello" when ssopp! Chippie got sucked in.

The bird owner gasped, put down the phone, turned off the vacuum and opened the bag. There was Chippie — still alive but stunned.

Since the bird was covered in dust she grabbed him and raced to the bathroom, turned on the tap, and held Chippie under the running water. Then, realizing that Chippie was soaked and shivering, she did what any compassionate bird owner would do — she reached for the hair dryer and blasted the pet with hot air.

Poor Chippie never knew what hit him.

A few days after the trauma, the reporter who'd initially written about the event contacted Chippie's owner to see how the bird was recovering. "Well," she replied, "Chippie doesn't sing much anymore — he just sits and stares."

It's not difficult to see why.

> *"These days, what isn't worth saying is sung."*
> **Pierre de Beaumarchais**

Sisters

Anthony came home from school one day, all banged up, bloodied, and bruised. His father asked him what on earth had happened.

"Well, dad, it's like this," Anthony began. "I challenged Eddie to a duel and you know how that goes… I gave him his choice of weapons."

"Uh huh," said the father. "That seems fair."

"I know… but I never thought he'd choose his sister!"

Skepticism

A newly converted hippie was intently reading the Bible while waiting for transportation and every now and then he would exclaim, "Alleluia, Praise the Lord, Amen" as he read on.

A skeptic heard him and came and asked what he was reading. He answered, "I am reading how God parted the Red Sea and let the Israelites go through — that is a miracle!" The skeptic said, "Do not believe everything the Bible tells you. The truth of the matter is that that body of water was only really six inches deep — so it was no miracle."

The hippie nodded in disappointment but kept on reading as the skeptic was walking away feeling proud that he had set the hippie straight.

All of a sudden the skeptic heard the hippie let out a big "Alleluia, Praise the Lord."

At this the skeptic came back to him and asked, "What is it this time?"

The hippie said excitedly in one breath, "This one is a real miracle, God drowned the whole Egyptian army in six inches of water!"

Slander

A man was sued by a woman for defamation of character. She charged that he had called her a pig. The man was found guilty and fined.

After the trial he asked the judge, "Does this mean that I cannot call Mrs Johnson a pig?"

The judge said that was true.

"Does this also mean I cannot call a pig, 'Mrs Johnson'?" the man asked.

The judge replied that he could indeed call a pig "Mrs Johnson" with no fear of legal action.

The man looked directly at Mrs Johnson and said, "Good afternoon, Mrs Johnson."

A minister was being constantly criticized by a member of his congregation.

After six months of this the poor man could stand it no more. He went out on a nice hot summer's afternoon for a drive in the countryside. He wound down the windows and after about an hour of driving began to feel much better.

Driving down a narrow country lane, however, he was horrified to see a car careering towards him out of control. As it approached, he realized with even greater horror that the lady driving the car was the very woman who had been harassing him.

As they passed within an inch of each other, the woman shouted the word "PIG!"

Months of built-up tension got the better of the minister and he shouted back, "COW!"

Then he drove round the corner and hit the pig.

Smile

A smile is a light in the window of a face which shows that the heart is at home.

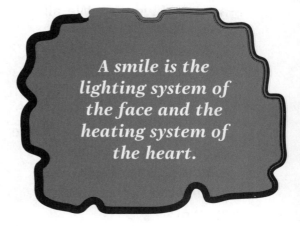

A smile is the lighting system of the face and the heating system of the heart.

All people smile in the same language.

A warm smile thaws an icy stare.

A smile is God's cosmetic.

Smile! It improves your face value!

Society

This is part of an address to those who are responsible for legislation in the US, including the law that bans prayer in schools…

On Thursday, 8 March 2001, Darrell Scott, the father of Rachel Scott, a victim of the Columbine High School shootings in Littleton, Colorado, was invited to address the House Judiciary Committee's subcommittee. This is part of what he said:

"Since the dawn of creation there has been both good and evil in the hearts of men and women. We all contain the seeds of kindness or the seeds of violence. The death of my wonderful daughter, Rachel Joy Scott, and the death of that heroic teacher, and the other eleven children who died must not be in vain. Their blood cries out for answers.

"I am here today to declare that Columbine was not just a tragedy — it was a spiritual event that should be forcing us to look at where the real blame lies! Much of the blame lies here in this room.

"I wrote a poem just four nights ago that expresses my feelings best. This was written before I knew I would be speaking here today:

Your laws ignore our
    deepest needs,
Your words are empty air.
You've stripped away our
    heritage,
You've outlawed simple
    prayer.
Now gunshots fill our
    classrooms,
And precious children die.
You seek for answers
    everywhere,
And ask the question
    "Why?"
You regulate restrictive
    laws,
Through legislative creed.

And yet you fail to
    understand,
That God is what we
    need!

"Men and women are
three-part beings. We all
consist of body, soul, and
spirit. When we refuse to
acknowledge a third part of
our makeup, we create a
void that allows evil,
prejudice, and hatred to
rush in and wreak havoc.

"Eric and Dylan would not
have been stopped by
metal detectors. No
amount of gun laws can
stop someone who spends
months planning this type
of massacre. The real villain
lies within our own hearts.
Political posturing and
restrictive legislation are
not the answers. The young
people of our nation hold
the key.

"As my son Craig lay
under that table in the
school library and saw his
two friends murdered
before his very eyes — he
did not hesitate to pray in
school. I defy any law or
politician to deny him that
right! I challenge every
young person in America,
and around the world, to
realize that on April 20,
1999, at Columbine High
School prayer was brought
back to our schools. Do not
let the many prayers
offered by those students
be in vain. My daughter's
death will not be in vain!
The young people of this
country will not allow that
to happen!"

Spontaneity

Spontaneity is a mixed blessing, as the following spontaneous comments from football commentators reveal:

"If plan A fails, they could always revert to plan A."
Mark Lawrenson

"I'm not going to look beyond the semi-final — but I'd love to lead Newcastle out at the final."
Bobby Robson

"Forest have now lost six matches without winning."
David Coleman

"I'm not saying David Ginola is the best winger in the Premiership, but there's none better."
Ron Atkinson

"Without being too harsh on David Beckham, he cost us the match."
Ian Wright

"Once you've had a bull terrier, you never want another dog. I've got six bull terriers, a rottweiler and a bulldog."
Julian Dicks

"Never go for a 50-50 ball unless you're 80-20 sure of winning it."
Ian Darke

"The referee has a reputation for trying to make a name for himself."
Graeme Souness

"Football today would certainly not be the same had it never existed."
Elton Welsby

"For those of you watching in black and white, Spurs are in the all-yellow strip."
John Motson

"Arsenal now have plenty of time to dictate the last few seconds."
Peter Jones

"Sporting Lisbon in their green and white hoops, looking like a team of Zebras."
Peter Jones

"He dribbles a lot, and the opposition don't like it — you can see it all over their faces."
Ron Atkinson

Storms

Did you know that an eagle knows when a storm is approaching long before it breaks?

The eagle will fly to some high spot and wait for the winds to come. When the storm hits, it sets its wings so that the wind will pick it up and lift it above the storm. While the storm rages below, the eagle is soaring above it. The eagle does not escape the storm. It simply uses the storm to lift it higher. It rises on the winds that bring the storm.

When the storms of life come upon us — and all of us will experience them — we can rise above them by setting our minds and our belief toward God. The storms do not have to overcome us. We can allow God's power to lift us above them.

God enables us to ride the winds of the storm that bring sickness, tragedy, failure and disappointment in our lives. We can soar above the storm.

Remember, it is not the burdens of life that weigh us down, it is how we handle them.

The Bible says, *"Those who hope in the Lord will renew their strength. They will soar on wings like eagles"* Isaiah 40:31.

Stubbornness

The duck hunter trained his retriever to walk on water. Eager to show off this amazing accomplishment, he asked a friend to go along on his next hunting trip. Saying nothing, he fired his first shot and, as the duck fell, the dog walked on the surface of the water, retrieved the duck and returned it to his master.

"Notice anything?" the owner asked eagerly.

"Yes," said his friend, "I see that fool dog of yours can't swim."

Students

Rejected Final Thesis Proposals

Spiritual Maturity: The Quick and Easy Method

Eight Characteristics of a Wealthy Church

Strategy for eliminating elders you don't like without confrontation

If I write 125 pages, will you give me the degree?

The Humble Minister's guide to accumulating power and authority

Legalism: A Misunderstood spiritual discipline

The Mocha Non-fat Latte: A Trinitarian metaphor for effective ministry

Tattoo Iconography: Cutting-edge Sunday School Curriculum

"I'm OK, You're OK": A guide to counseling in the local church

Voice answering systems: Creative strategies for avoiding problem people

Preaching without preparation: Why quench the Spirit?

Winner Takes All: Becoming the leader you were meant to be

Suffering

"God does not bring about everything that happens in the world. Because God is a God of love, he allows creatures to be themselves and to make themselves. That sort of valuable, worthwhile, independent creation has a cost. We see that in the terrible cruel choices of humankind. We also see it in the physical history of the world. Exactly the same bio-chemical processes that enable some cells to mutate and produce new forms of life — the very engine that has driven the amazingly fruitful history of life on earth — will allow other cells to mutate and to become malignant. You just cannot have one without the other. The tragic fact that there is cancer in the world is not because God did not bother — it is a necessity in a world allowed to make itself."

John Polkinghorne, Professor of Mathematical Physics at Cambridge University

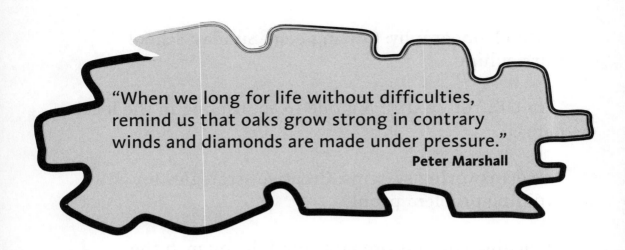

"When we long for life without difficulties, remind us that oaks grow strong in contrary winds and diamonds are made under pressure."

Peter Marshall

Superstition

"I'm not a practising Christian, but I pray. I read the Bible. It's the most beautiful book ever written. I should go to heaven, otherwise it's not nice. I haven't done anything wrong. My conscience is very clean. My soul is as white as those orchids over there, and I should go straight, straight to heaven."

Sophia Loren

Surprises

A taxi passenger tapped the driver on the shoulder to ask him something. The driver screamed, lost control of the car, nearly hit a bus, went up on the pavement, and stopped centimeters from a shop window.

For a second everything went quiet in the cab, then the driver said, "Look mister, don't ever do that again. You scared the daylights out of me!"

The passenger apologized and said he didn't realize that a little tap could scare him so much.

The driver replied "Sorry, it's not really your fault. Today is my first day as a cab driver. I've been driving hearses for the last 25 years."

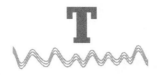

T

Tact

> *Tact is changing the subject without changing your mind.*

One office supervisor called a secretary in to give her the bad news that she was being fired.

He started the conversation with:

"Miss Smythe, I really don't know how we're going to get along without you, but starting Monday, we're going to try."

A Regimental Sergeant Major (RSM, a fearsome army character with a loud voice) is drilling some recruits on the parade ground when he gets a message that the mother of one of them has died.

(RSM) "SMITH, YOUR MOTHER'S DEAD!" Smith drops down in a dead faint.

The RSM's superior officer takes him to one side afterwards and tells him he should be a bit more tactful about such things.

(RSM) "YES, SIR, I WILL BE."

A week later a similar event occurs.

(RSM, on the parade ground) "ALL THOSE WITH MOTHERS, TWO STEPS FORWARD!"

"JONES, WHERE DO YOU THINK YOU'RE GOING?"

Talk

I thought talk was cheap until I saw our telephone bill.

Some people would say more if they talked less.

Temptation

There's always fresh cheese in the mousetrap.

One of the best illustrations of the progressive nature of temptation can be found in the *Jungle Doctor* stories. The story in question is called "The Small Wisdom of Feeding Vultures".

A small monkey called Tichi was once fascinated by the curves of the dangerous beaks of vultures. A vulture landed near Tichi in the family tree. Tichi stared at every inch of its foul body. When no one was looking he threw it some food, then clapped and shouted "Be Gone!" Next day two vultures came and landed near Tichi. Again he threw food to the vultures before clapping and shouting "Be Gone!" Soon more and more came to the tree and Tichi was now scared so he started to throw stones at the big birds.

As the week went by the vultures no longer stood at a distance from Tichi. They grew bolder and bolder and drew closer and closer. Some were above the little monkey. Some were below. More and more began to circle ahead. Tichi started to clap and scream frantically. But eventually there were too many. The vultures alighted and there was one final shrill cry as the monkey was devoured.

Such is the danger of any fascination with sin.

Thanksgiving

A Jewish Passover Prayer:

"Even if our mouths were filled with songs like the sea, our tongues with joy like its mighty waves, our lips with praise like the breadth of the sky, if our eyes shone like the sun and the moon, and our hands were spread out like the eagles of heaven, if our feet were as swift as the hind, we should still be incapable of thanking you adequately for one thousandth part of all the love You have shown us."

"If the only prayer you said in your whole life was, 'thank you', that would suffice."
Meister Eckhart

Time

"Time is the wisest of all counselors."
Plutarch

If you think time heals everything, try waiting in a doctor's surgery.

Our days are identical suitcases — all the same size — but some people can pack more into them than others.

Sign on a school clock: "Time will pass. Will you?"

Counting time is not as important as making time count.

If I knew it would be the last time that I'd see you fall asleep, I would tuck you in more tightly, and pray the Lord your soul to keep.

If I knew it would be the last time that I saw you walk out the door, I would give you a hug and kiss, and call you back for one more.

If I knew it would be the last time I'd hear your voice lifted up in praise, I would videotape each word, so I could play them back day after day.

If I knew it would be the last time, I could spare an extra minute or two to stop and say "I love you", instead of assuming you would KNOW I do.

If I knew it would be the last time I would be there to share your day, well I'm sure you'll have so many more, so I can let just this one slip away.

For surely there's always tomorrow to make up for an oversight, and we always get a second chance to make everything right.

There will always be another day to say our "I love you's", and certainly there's another chance to say our "Anything I can do?"

But just in case I might be wrong, and today is all I get, I'd like to say how much I love you and I hope we never forget.

Tomorrow is not promised to anyone, young or old alike. And today may be the last chance you get to hold your loved one tight…

So if you're waiting for tomorrow, why not do it today?

For if tomorrow never comes, you'll surely regret the day, that you didn't take that extra time for a smile, a hug, or a kiss, and you were too busy to grant someone what turned out to be their one last wish.

So hold your loved ones close today, whisper in their ear, tell them how much you love them and that you'll always hold them dear.

Take time to say "I'm sorry", "please forgive me", "thank you" or "it's okay". And if tomorrow never comes, you'll have no regrets about today.

Kodak gives you pictures of yesterday
Polaroid gives you pictures of today
But only God can give you pictures of tomorrow!

Troubles

I hired a plumber to help me restore an old farmhouse, and after he had just finished a rough first day on the job, a flat tire made him lose an hour of work and his electric drill quit. Then his ancient one-ton truck refused to start. As I drove him home, he sat in stony silence.

On arriving he invited me in to meet his family. As we walked towards the front door, he paused briefly at a small tree, touching the tips of the branches with both hands. Upon opening the door he had undergone an amazing transformation. His tanned face was wreathed in smiles and he hugged his two small children and gave his wife a kiss.

Afterward he walked me to the car. We passed the tree and my curiosity got the better of me. I asked him about what I had seen him do at the little tree.

"Oh, that's my trouble tree," he replied. "I know I can't help having troubles on the job, but one thing's for sure, those troubles don't belong in the house with my wife and the children. So I just hang them up on the tree every night when I come home and ask God to take care of them. Then in the morning I pick them up again. Funny thing is," he smiled, "when I come out in the morning to pick them up, there aren't nearly as many as I remember hanging up the night before."

"The ultimate measure of a person is not where they stand in moments of comfort and convenience, but where they stand at times of challenge and controversy."

Dr Martin Luther King, Jr

Truth

"Truth is not a virtue unless it is given with love!"

Pete Welsh

Beware of half-truths. You may have got hold of the wrong half!

It is better to be:
divided by truth, than united in error;
to speak the truth that hurts and then heals, than to speak
  a lie that will comfort and then kill;
to be hated for telling the truth than to be loved for telling
  a lie;
to stand alone with the truth than to be wrong with a
  multitude;
to die ultimately with the truth, than to live with a lie.

Understanding

"One understands people through the heart, not the eyes or the intellect."

Mark Twain

The best way to be understood is to be understanding.

I hear, I forget; I see, I remember; I do, I understand.

Unity

There was once an old monastery that had fallen upon hard times. Centuries earlier it had been a thriving monastery where many dedicated monks lived and worked and had great influence, but now only five monks lived there and they were all over 70 years old. This was clearly a dying order.

A few miles from the monastery lived an old hermit who many thought was a prophet. One day as the monks agonized over the impending demise of their order, they decided to visit the hermit to see if he might have some advice for them. Perhaps he would be able to see the future and show them what they could do to save the monastery.

The hermit welcomed the five monks to his hut, but when they explained the purpose of their visit he could only commiserate with them. "Yes I understand how it is," said the hermit, "the spirit has gone out of the people, hardly anyone cares much for the old things anymore."

"Is there anything you can tell us," the Abbot enquired of the hermit, "that could help us to save the monastery?"

"No I am sorry," said the hermit. "I don't know how your monastery can be saved, the only thing that I can tell you is that one of you is an Apostle of God."

The monks were both disappointed and confused by the hermit's cryptic statement. They returned to the monastery wondering what the hermit could have meant by the statement "one of you is an Apostle of God". For months after their visit, the monks pondered the significance of the hermit's words.

"One of us is an Apostle of God," they mused. "Did he actually mean, one of us monks here at the monastery? That is impossible. We are all too old, we are all too insignificant. On the other hand, what if it is true and if it is true, then which one of us is it?

"Do you suppose he meant the Abbot? Yes, if he meant anyone, he probably meant the Abbot. He has been our leader for more than a generation. On the other hand he might have meant Brother Thomas. Certainly Brother Thomas is a holy man, a man of wisdom and light. He couldn't have meant Brother Elred. Elred gets crochety at times and is difficult to reason with. On the other hand, he is almost always right. Maybe the hermit did meant Brother Elred. But surely he could not have meant Brother Philip? Brother Philip is so passive, so shy, a real nobody. Still, he is always there when you need him. He is loyal and trustworthy. Yes, he could have meant Philip. Of course the hermit didn't mean me, he couldn't possibly have meant me. I am just an ordinary person. Yet suppose he did. Suppose I am an Apostle of God. Oh God, not me. I couldn't be that much for you. Or could I?"

As they contemplated in this manner, the old monks began to treat each other with extraordinary respect on the off chance that one of them might actually be an Apostle of God and on the off, off chance that each monk himself might be the apostle spoken of by the hermit, each monk began to treat himself with extraordinary respect.

Because the monastery was situated in a beautiful forest, many people came there to picnic on its lawn and to walk on its paths and now and then to go into the tiny chapel to meditate. As they did so, without even being conscious of it, they sensed the aura of extraordinary respect that now began to surround the five old monks and seemed to radiate from them, permeating the atmosphere of the place. There was something strangely attractive, even compelling, about it. Hardly knowing why, people began to bring their friends to show them this special place, and their friends brought their friends.

As more and more visitors came, some of the younger men started to talk with the old monks. After a while one asked if he could join them, then another, then another. Within a few years, the monastery had once again become a thriving order and thanks to the hermit's wisdom a vibrant center of light and spirituality throughout the region.

Weak things united become strong.

"None of us has got it together, but together we've got it."
J. John

"If a link is broken, the whole chain breaks."
Yiddish proverb

Valentine

A vegetarian's Valentine message

Cabbage always has a heart; Green beans string along. You're such a Tomato, Will you Peas to me belong?

You've been the Apple of my eye, You know how much I care; So Lettuce get together, We'd make a perfect Pear.

Now, something's sure to Turnip, To prove you can't be Beet; So, if you Carrot all for me Let's let our Tulips meet.

Don't Squash my hopes and dreams now, Bee my Honey, dear; Or tears will fill Potato's eyes, While Sweet Corn lends an ear.

I'll Cauliflower shop and say Your dreams are Parsley mine. I'll work and share my Celery, So be my Valentine.

Vanity

A middle-aged woman has a heart attack. While on the operating table she has a near-death experience. She sees God, and asks if this is it. God says no, that she has another 30 years to live. She recovers, and decides to stay in the hospital and have a facelift, liposuction, tummy tuck, etc. She figures since she's got another 30 years she might as well make the most of it.

She walks out of the hospital after the last operation and immediately gets hit by an ambulance. She arrives in front of God and asks, "I thought you said I had another 30 years?"

God replies, "I didn't recognize you."

Vets

A man runs into the vet's office carrying his dog, screaming for help. The vet has him put his dog down on the examination table. The vet examines the still, limp body and after a few moments tells the man that his dog, regrettably, is dead.

The man, clearly agitated and not willing to accept this, demands a second opinion. The vet goes into the back room and comes out with a cat and puts the cat down next to the dog's body. The cat sniffs the body, walks from head to tail poking and sniffing the dog's body and finally looks at the vet and meows. The vet looks at the man and says, "I'm sorry, but the cat thinks that your dog is dead too."

The man is still unwilling to accept that his dog is dead. The vet brings in a black labrador. The lab sniffs the body, walks from head to tail, and finally looks at the vet and barks. The vet looks at the man and says, "I'm sorry, but the lab thinks your dog is dead too."

The man, finally resigned to the diagnosis, thanks the vet and asks how much he owes.

The vet answers, "£300."

"£300 to tell me my dog is dead?" exclaimed the man.

"Well," the vet replies, "I would only have charged you £25 for my initial diagnosis. The additional £250 was for the cat scan and lab tests."

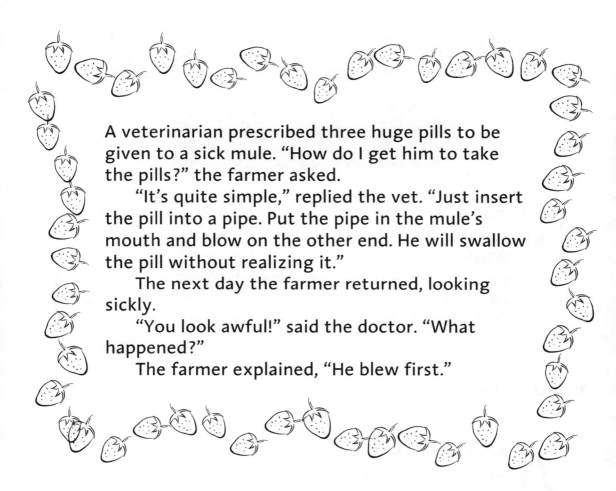

A veterinarian prescribed three huge pills to be given to a sick mule. "How do I get him to take the pills?" the farmer asked.

"It's quite simple," replied the vet. "Just insert the pill into a pipe. Put the pipe in the mule's mouth and blow on the other end. He will swallow the pill without realizing it."

The next day the farmer returned, looking sickly.

"You look awful!" said the doctor. "What happened?"

The farmer explained, "He blew first."

Vision

"Always remember that this whole thing started with a mouse."

Walt Disney

"The further backward you can look, the further forward you are likely to see."

Winston Churchill

"Vision is the art of seeing things invisible."

Jonathan Swift

What's the use of running if you're on the wrong road?

A tourist visiting Italy came upon a construction site.
  "What are you doing?" he asked three stonemasons.
  "I'm cutting the stone," answered the first.
  "I'm cutting stone for 1,000 lire a day," the second said.
  "I'm helping to build a cathedral," said the third.

Vulnerability

A water bearer in India had two large pots, one hung on each end of a pole which he carried across his neck. One of the pots had a crack in it, and while the other pot was perfect and always delivered a full portion of water at the end of the long walk from the stream to the master's house, the cracked pot arrived only half full. For two years this went on daily, with the bearer delivering only one and a half pots full of water to his master's house. Of course, the perfect pot was proud of its accomplishments, perfect to the end for which it was made. But the poor cracked pot was ashamed of its own imperfection, and miserable that it was able to accomplish only half of what it had been created to do.

After two years of what it perceived to be bitter failure, it spoke to the water bearer one day by the stream. "I am ashamed of myself, and I want to apologize to you." "Why?" asked the bearer. "What are you ashamed of?" "I have been able, for these past two years, to deliver only half my load because this crack in my side causes water to leak out all the way back to your master's house. Because of my flaws, you have to do all of this work, and you don't get full value from your efforts," the pot said.

The water bearer felt sorry for the old cracked pot, and in his compassion he said, "As we return to the master's house, I want you to notice the beautiful flowers along the path." Indeed, as they went up the hill, the old cracked pot took notice of the sun warming the beautiful wild flowers on the side of the path, and this cheered it some. But at the end of the trail, it still felt bad because it had leaked out half its load, and so again it apologized to the bearer for its failure.

The bearer said to the pot, "Did you notice that there were flowers only on your side of your path, but not on the other pot's side? That's because I have always known about your flaw, and I took advantage of it. I planted flower seeds on your side of the path, and every day while we walk back from the stream, you've watered them. For two years I have been able to pick these beautiful flowers to decorate my master's table. Without you being just the way you are, he would not have this beauty to grace his house."

On 18 November 1995, Itzhak Perlman, the violinst, came on stage to give a concert at Avery Fisher Hall at Lincoln Center in New York City. If you have ever been to a Perlman concert, you know that getting on stage is no small achievement for him. He was stricken with polio as a child, and so he has braces on both legs and walks with the aid of two crutches.

To see him walk across the stage one step at a time, painfully and slowly, is an unforgettable sight. He walks painfully, yet majestically, until he reaches his chair. Then he sits down, slowly, puts his crutches on the floor, undoes the clasps on his legs, tucks one foot back and extends the other foot forward. Then he bends down and picks up the violin, puts it under his chin, nods to the conductor and proceeds to play.

By now, the audience is used to this ritual. They sit quietly while he makes his way across the stage to his chair. They remain reverently silent while he undoes the clasps on his legs. They wait until he is ready to play.

But this time, something went wrong. Just as he finished the first few bars, one of the strings on his violin broke. You could hear it snap — it went off like gunfire across the room. There was no mistaking what that sound meant.

There was no mistaking what he had to do. People who were there that night thought to themselves:

"We figured that he would have to get up, put on the clasps again, pick up the crutches and limp his way off stage — to either find another violin or else find another string for this one."

But he didn't. Instead, he waited a moment, closed his eyes and then he played with such passion and such power and such purity as they had never heard before. Of course, anyone knows that it is impossible to play a symphonic work with just three strings. I know that, and you know that, but that night Itzhak Perlman refused to know that.

You could see him modulating, changing, recomposing the piece in his head. At one point, it sounded like he was de-tuning the strings to get new sounds from them that they had never made before.

When he finished, there was an awesome silence in the room. And then people rose and cheered. There was an extraordinary outburst of applause from every corner of the auditorium. We were all on our feet, screaming and cheering, doing everything we could to show how much we appreciated what he had done.

He smiled, wiped the sweat from his brow, raised his bow to quiet us, and then he said, not boastfully, but in a quiet, pensive, reverent tone, "You know, sometimes it is the artist's task to find out how much music you can still make with what you have left."

Women

Nine reasons why God created Eve:

- God was worried that Adam would get lost in the garden and would not ask for directions
- God knew that one day Adam would need someone to help him find the remote
- God knew Adam would never go out by himself and buy a new fig leaf
- God knew Adam would never make a doctor's or dentist's appointment on his own
- God knew Adam would never remember which night to put out the rubbish
- God knew Adam would never handle the responsibility of childbirth
- God knew Adam would need help locating his gardening implements
- God knew Adam would need someone else to blame
- God finished making Adam, scratched his head and said, "I can do better than that!"

A man walked into a bookstore and asked the woman behind the counter, "Have you got a book called, 'Man, the Master of Women'?"

"Try the fiction section," said the woman.

What Women Want in a Man, Original List (age 22)

1. Handsome; 2. Charming; 3. Financially successful;
4. A caring listener; 5. Witty; 6. In good shape;
7. Dresses with style; 8. Appreciates finer things;
9. Full of thoughtful surprises; 10. An imaginative,
romantic lover.

What Women Want in a Man, Revised List (age 32)

1. Nice looking (prefer hair on his head); 2. Opens car
doors, holds chairs; 3. Has enough money for a nice
dinner; 4. Listens more than talks; 5. Laughs at my
jokes; 6. Carries bags of groceries with ease; 7. Owns
at least one tie; 8. Appreciates a good home-cooked
meal; 9. Remembers birthdays and anniversaries;
10. Seeks romance at least once a week.

What Women Want in a Man, Revised List (age 42)

1. Not too ugly (bald head OK); 2. Doesn't drive off
until I'm in the car; 3. Works steadily — splurges on
dinner out occasionally; 4. Nods head when I'm
talking; 5. Usually remembers punch lines of jokes;
6. Is in good enough shape to rearrange the furniture;
7. Wears a shirt that covers his stomach; 8. Knows not
to buy champagne with screw-top lids; 9. Remembers
to put the toilet seat down; 10. Shaves most weekends.

What Women Want in a Man, Revised List (age 52)

1. Keeps hair in nose and ears trimmed; 2. Doesn't belch or scratch in public; 3. Doesn't borrow money too often; 4. Doesn't nod off to sleep when I'm venting; 5. Doesn't re-tell the same joke too many times; 6. Is in good enough shape to get off couch on weekends; 7. Usually wears matching socks and fresh underwear; 8. Appreciates a good TV dinner; 9. Remembers your name on occasion; 10. Shaves some weekends.

What Women Want in a Man, Revised List (age 62)

1. Doesn't scare small children; 2. Remembers where bathroom is; 3. Doesn't require much money for upkeep; 4. Only snores lightly when asleep; 5. Remembers why he's laughing; 6. Is in good enough shape to stand up by himself; 7. Usually wears some clothes; 8. Likes soft foods; 9. Remembers where he left his teeth; 10. Remembers that it's the weekend.

What Women Want in a Man, Revised List (age 72)

Breathing

World

"*The most incomprehensible thing about the world is that it is incomprehensible.*"

Albert Einstein

Worry

Fresh out of business school, the young man answered an advertisement for an accountant. Now he was being interviewed by a very stressed man who ran a small business that he had started himself.

"I need someone with an accounting degree," the man said. "But mainly, I'm looking for someone to do my worrying for me."

"Excuse me?" the accountant said.

"I worry about a lot of things," the man said. "But I don't want to have to worry about money. Your job will be to take all the money worries off my back."

"I see," the accountant said. "And how much does the job pay?"

"I'll start you at 80 thousand."

"Eighty thousand dollars!" the accountant exclaimed. "How can such a small business afford a sum like that?"

"That," the owner said, "is your first worry."

Worship

"To worship is…
to quicken the conscience by the holiness of God,
to feed the mind with the truth of God,
to purge the imagination by the beauty of God,
to open the heart to the love of God,
to devote the will to the purpose of God."

William Temple

"Christian worship is the most urgent, the most glorious action that takes place in human life."

Karl Barth

"Wash your face every morning in a bath of praise."

Charles Spurgeon

God wants to receive back his own flowers as gifts from people's hands.

"A drop of praise is an unsuitable acknowledgement for an ocean of mercy."

William Secker

"God prefers bad verses recited with a pure heart to the finest verses chanted by the wicked."

Voltaire

Xmas Files

By R. Birsch

57 ELM STREET BETHLEHEM, PA. 11.51 PM, 24 DECEMBER
"We're too late! It's already been here."

"Mulder, I hope you know what you're doing."

"Look, Scully, just like the other homes: Douglas fir, truncated, mounted, transformed into a shrine; halls decked with boughs of holly; stockings hung by the chimney, with care."

"You really think someone's been here?"

"Someone…or something."

"Mulder, over here — it's a fruitcake."

"Don't touch it! Those things can be lethal."

"It's OK. There's a note attached: 'Gonna find out who's naughty and nice.'"

"It's judging them, Scully. It's making a list."

"Who? What are you talking about?"

"Ancient mythology tells of an obese humanoid entity who could travel at great speed in a craft powered by antlered servants. Once each year, near the winter solstice, this creature is said to descend from the heavens to reward its followers and punish disbelievers with jagged chunks of anthracite. But that's legend, Mulder — a story told by parents to frighten children. Surely you don't believe it?"

"Something was here tonight, Scully. Check out the bite marks on this gingerbread man. Whatever tore through this plate of cookies was massive — and in a hurry."

"It left crumbs everywhere. And look, Mulder, this milk glass has been completely drained."

"It gorged itself, Scully. It fed without remorse."

"But why would they leave it milk and cookies?"

"Appeasement. Tonight is the Eve, and nothing can stop its wilding."

"But if this thing does exist, how did it get in? The doors and windows were locked. There's no sign of forced entry."

"Unless I miss my guess, it came through the fireplace."

"Wait a minute, Mulder. If you're saying some huge creature landed on the roof and came down this chimney, you're crazy. The flue is barely six inches wide. Nothing could get down there."

"But what if it could alter its shape, move in all directions at once?"

"You mean, like a bowl full of jelly?"

"Exactly. Scully, I've never told anyone this, but when I was a child my home was visited. I saw the creature. It had long white shanks of fur surrounding its ruddy, misshapen head. Its bloated torso was red and white. I'll never forget the horror. I turned away, and when I looked back it had somehow taken on the facial features of my father."

"Impossible."

"I know what I saw. And that night it read my mind. It brought me a Mr Potato Head, Scully. It knew that I wanted a Mr Potato Head!"

"I'm sorry, Mulder, but you're asking me to disregard the laws of physics. You want me to believe in some supernatural being who soars across the skies and brings gifts to good little girls and boys. Listen to what you're saying. Do you understand the repercussions? If this gets out, they'll close the X-files."

"Scully, listen to me: It knows when you're sleeping. It knows when you're awake. But we have no proof."

"Last year, on this exact date, SETI radio telescopes detected bogeys in the airspace over 27 states. The White House ordered a Condition Red. But that was a meteor shower."

"Officially. Two days ago, eight prized Scandinavian reindeer vanished from the National Zoo, in Washington DC. Nobody — not even the zookeeper — was told about it. The government doesn't want people to know about Project Kringle. They fear that if this thing is proved to exist the public will stop spending half its annual income in a holiday shopping frenzy. Retail markets will collapse. Scully, they cannot let the world believe this creature lives. There's too much at stake. They'll do whatever it takes to insure another silent night."

"Mulder, I — "

"Sh-h-h. Do you hear what I hear?"

"On the roof. It sounds like…a clatter."

"The truth is up there. Let's see what's the matter."

Y

Youth

A teenage girl had been talking on the phone for about half an hour, and then she hung up.

"Wow!" said her father, "That was short. You usually talk for two hours. What happened?"

"Wrong number," replied the girl.

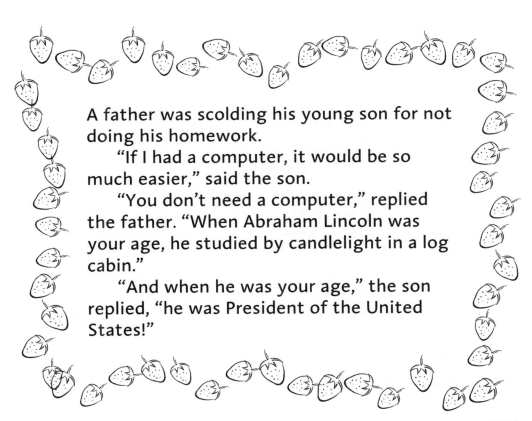

A father was scolding his young son for not doing his homework.

"If I had a computer, it would be so much easier," said the son.

"You don't need a computer," replied the father. "When Abraham Lincoln was your age, he studied by candlelight in a log cabin."

"And when he was your age," the son replied, "he was President of the United States!"

A teenage girl had been talking on the phone for about half an hour, and then she hung up.

"Wow," said her father. "That was short. You usually talk for two hours. What happened?"

"Wrong number," replied the girl.

A father was scolding his young son for not doing his homework.

"If I had a computer, it would be so much easier," said the son.

"You don't need a computer," replied the father. "When Abraham Lincoln was your age, he studied by candlelight in a log cabin."

"And when he was your age," the son replied, "he was President of the United States."

Z

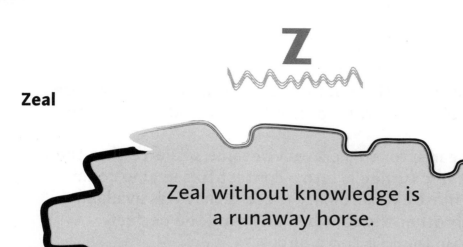

Zeal

Zeal without knowledge is a runaway horse.

Zest

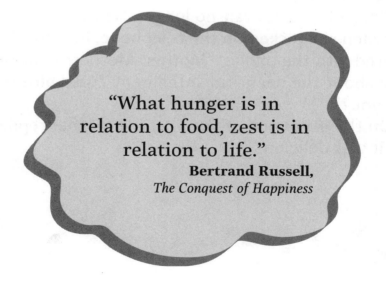

"What hunger is in relation to food, zest is in relation to life."
Bertrand Russell,
The Conquest of Happiness

Zurka bird

Two wealthy brothers set out one Christmas to purchase the very best Christmas present they could find for their mother.

The search for this present became so fierce that the two brothers turned it into a contest to see who could find the most extraordinary present that was available.

One brother thought he had found the perfect present. He found a Zurka bird.

The Zurka bird was no ordinary bird. It was a very rare and special bird. It was very expensive, had to be flown in from the Amazon. It could speak five different languages. It could recite poetry and sing opera. It was an amazing bird.

So one brother paid dearly for the Zurka bird, and had it sent to his mother for Christmas.

Finally he could wait no longer. He called his mother and when she picked up the telephone, he almost shouted into the phone, "Mother, Mother, what did you think about the beautiful, intelligent Zurka bird that I sent you?"

On the other end of the line, the Mother replied, "Oh son, it was delicious."